U.S. Policy Toward
the Korean Peninsula

COUNCIL *on*
FOREIGN
RELATIONS

Independent Task Force Report No. 64

Charles L. Pritchard and John H. Tilelli Jr.,
Chairs
Scott A. Snyder, *Project Director*

U.S. Policy Toward
the Korean Peninsula

Task Force Members

Task Force members are asked to join a consensus signifying that they endorse "the general policy thrust and judgments reached by the group, though not necessarily every finding and recommendation." They participate in the Task Force in their individual, not institutional, capacities.

Michael R. Auslin

Douglas K. Bereuter

Victor D. Cha

Charles B. Curtis

Nicholas Eberstadt

Robert L. Gallucci

Michael J. Green

Stephan Haggard

Siegfried S. Hecker

Fred C. Iklé

Charles Jones

William J. Lennox Jr.

Marcus Noland

Don Oberdorfer

Michael O'Hanlon

Jonathan D. Pollack

Charles L. Pritchard

Evans J.R. Revere

Stanley Owen Roth

James J. Shinn

Susan L. Shirk

Scott A. Snyder

John H. Tilelli Jr.

Contents

Foreword

It is one of the last remaining geopolitical problems of the twentieth century: a divided peninsula occupied by two countries still technically at war—one dynamic and modern, the other closed, impoverished, and belligerent. The countries, of course, are the two Koreas, and the peninsula they share represents one of the most vexing challenges facing the world today.

The gravest threat is North Korea's nuclear program. The North's nuclear arsenal, its pursuit of more advanced missile technology, and the possibility that it could transfer nuclear weapons or materials to others (whether states or terrorist groups) pose significant dangers to the United States and its allies in the region and beyond. Successive U.S. administrations have struggled, largely unsuccessfully, to address this set of dangers. In particular, the Six Party Talks—consisting of China, Japan, North Korea, Russia, South Korea, and the United States—have failed to bring about North Korea's denuclearization. The Council on Foreign Relations wrestled with issues involving the Korean peninsula in five separate Independent Task Force reports between 1995 and 2003, and it has now done so again in 2010, indicating both the seriousness of the problems and the lack of progress in resolving them.

The urgency of the threat is undeniable. North Korea possesses nuclear-weapon and missile capabilities, has threatened its neighbors, and has been willing to sell nuclear materials and technology to the highest bidder. Its reclusive leadership is unpredictable, something yet again underscored by the unprovoked destruction of the *Cheonan*, a South Korean naval vessel, by a North Korean torpedo in late March 2010. Moreover, the future of its regime is uncertain, with the potential for a contested succession or breakdown of authority after the death of Kim Jong-il.

But while the danger is clear, progress is elusive. North Korea has boycotted nuclear disarmament talks since 2008, and their future is now in doubt after the sinking of the *Cheonan* and the resulting loss of forty-six South Korean lives. Moreover, it is far from obvious what the Six Party Talks could accomplish in the way of denuclearization even if they should resume.

This Task Force report comprehensively reviews the situation on the peninsula as well as the options for U.S. policy. It provides a valuable ranking of U.S. interests, and calls for a firm commitment from the Obama administration to seek denuclearization of the Korean peninsula, backed by a combination of sanctions, incentives, and sustained political pressure, in addition to increased efforts to contain proliferation. It notes that China's participation in this effort is vital. Indeed, the report makes clear that any hope of North Korea's dismantling its nuclear program rests on China's willingness to take a strong stance. For denuclearization to proceed, China must acknowledge that the long-term hazard of a nuclear Korea is more perilous to it and the region than the short-term risk of instability. The report also recognizes that robust relations between Washington and its allies in the region, Japan and South Korea, must underpin any efforts to deal with the North Korean problem.

It is also worth noting that the report does not stop at calling for the resumption of the Six Party Talks and additional diplomacy to bring about denuclearization. It looks as well at regime change and scenarios that could lead to reunification of the peninsula. There could be opportunities to make progress toward denuclearization or, with time, even reunification after Kim Jong-il departs from the scene. Again, though, China's role is likely to prove critical.

At the same time that the Task Force emphasizes the danger and urgency of North Korea's behavior, it recognizes and applauds the beneficial U.S. relationship with South Korea, which has proved to be a valuable economic and strategic partner. In this vein, the Task Force advocates continued close coordination with Seoul and urges prompt congressional passage of the U.S.-South Korea free trade agreement.

On behalf of the Council on Foreign Relations, I thank the Task Force chairs, Jack Pritchard and John Tilelli, and the individual Task Force members and observers, who all contributed their significant experience and expertise to this thoughtful report. I also urge readers to review the additional and dissenting views written by several Task Force members.

My thanks go as well to Task Force Program Director Anya Schmemann, who guided this project from start to finish, and to Adjunct
Senior Fellow Scott Snyder for ably and patiently directing the project and drafting the report. The Task Force took on one of the world's
knottiest and most protracted challenges and produced an important
study that helps to underscore the severity of the threat and the high
costs of inaction.

Richard N. Haass
President
Council on Foreign Relations
June 2010

Acknowledgments

The report of the Independent Task Force on U.S. Policy Toward the Korean Peninsula is the product of much work and effort by the dedicated members and observers of the Task Force, and I am appreciative of the time and attention they devoted to this project. In particular, I thank our distinguished chairs, Charles L. "Jack" Pritchard and John H. Tilelli Jr., for their leadership. It has been a pleasure to work with them and to travel with them to Seoul.

I am thankful to several people who met with me and various representatives of the Task Force, including Stephen W. Bosworth and Wendy Cutler, who briefed the Task Force on the Obama administration's positions. South Korean ambassador Han Duck-soo has also been gracious and helpful.

The report also benefited from consultations with experts and officials in the region. I am grateful to the Seoul Forum for International Affairs, especially Chairman Hongkoo Lee, Kim Daljoong, and Kim Sunghan, for arranging to host a workshop in Seoul on October 28, 2009, in conjunction with a parallel task force effort that they convened on the Korean side. I am particularly grateful to the Korea Foundation and its former president, Ambassador Yim Sung-joon, for generously supporting this project.

The chairs and I met with several officials in Seoul, including Ambassador Wi Sunglac, Defense Minister Kim Tae-young, and Foreign Minister Yu Myung-hwan, as well as U.S. ambassador Kathleen Stephens and U.S. Forces Korea commander Walter L. "Skip" Sharp. In addition, Ambassador Pritchard and I traveled separately to Pyongyang along with Nicole Finneman of the Korean Economic Institute and met with the Democratic People's Republic of Korea (DPRK) director general for North American affairs Ri Gun and several Ministry of Trade officials, including Hyon Chol, head of the Korean Foreign Investment Board.

The Task Force also received helpful input from many CFR members. The Washington Meetings team organized an event with CFR members in Washington, led by Task Force member Marcus Noland; the New York Meetings team organized an event for CFR members in New York, led by Task Force member James J. Shinn; and the National Program team organized a series of sessions with CFR members on the West Coast, led by Task Force member Stephan Haggard and CFR members David W. Lyon and Greyson L. Bryan.

I am grateful to many at CFR: CFR's Publications team assisted in editing the report and readied it for publication. CFR's Communications, Corporate, External Affairs, and Outreach teams all worked to ensure that the report reaches the widest audience possible.

Anya Schmemann and Kristin Lewis of CFR's Task Force Program were instrumental to this project from beginning to end, from the selection of Task Force members to the convening of meetings to the careful editing of multiple drafts. I am indebted to them for their assistance and for keeping me on track. I would also like to thank Nellie Dunderdale, Joyce Lee, and particularly See-Won Byun for their research in support of the Task Force report.

I am grateful to CFR President Richard N. Haass, Director of Studies James M. Lindsay, and former director of studies Gary S. Samore for giving me the opportunity to direct this effort. In addition to the Korea Foundation, the members thank David M. Rubenstein for his support of the Task Force Program.

While this report is the product of the Task Force, I take responsibility for its content and note that any omissions or mistakes are mine. Once again, my sincere thanks to all who contributed to this effort.

Scott A. Snyder
Project Director

Task Force Report

Introduction

The Korean peninsula simultaneously offers dramatically contrasting opportunities for and dangers to U.S. interests in Northeast Asia. On the one hand, a democratic and free market–oriented South Korea has developed enhanced military capacity and political clout and an expanded set of shared interests with the United States. This enables more active cooperation with the United States to respond to North Korea's nuclear challenge and promote regional and global stability and prosperity. On the other hand, a secretive and totalitarian North Korea has expanded its capacity to threaten regional and global stability through continued development of fissile materials and missile delivery capabilities, and has directly challenged the global nonproliferation regime and U.S. leadership.

The challenge posed by North Korea's nuclear development effort has global, regional, and bilateral dimensions. An internationally coordinated response must take all facets of the challenge into account. This Task Force report identifies three essential elements: first, denuclearization of the Korean peninsula and an approach that attempts to resolve rather than simply manage the issue; second, regional cohesion, enabled by close U.S.-South Korea relations; and, third, China's cooperation and active engagement.

Given the high level of mistrust between the United States and North Korea, the United States will not be able to change the situation by itself. It will need cooperation from counterparts in Asia who have already affirmed their support—through the Six Party Joint Statement of September 19, 2005—for the objectives of denuclearization, improved bilateral relations in the region, regional economic development, and the establishment of peace on the Korean peninsula.[1] The United States, China, Russia, South Korea, Japan, and North Korea have all signed on to this statement. The goal of the Obama administration should be to work with its partners to pursue its full implementation.

The United States and its partners have divergent interests and priorities regarding the North Korean challenge. China is more narrowly focused on the regional dimension and prioritizes stability. South Korea and Russia support denuclearization but want to achieve that objective by peaceful means. For Japan, the issue of how to deal with Japanese citizens abducted by North Korea in the 1970s has been a higher priority than denuclearization. The United States is understandably concerned about the global implications of Korea's nuclear program, the consequences for the global nonproliferation regime, and the potential spread of weapons, materials, and know-how to rogue states, terrorist groups, or others—especially in the Middle East. These different approaches and priorities were highlighted in the early responses to the March 2010 sinking of the South Korean warship *Cheonan*; the United States and South Korea implicated North Korea and have taken a tough approach designed to punish the North Korean regime, while China—worried about further escalation—has downplayed the incident.

A strong U.S.-South Korea alliance remains the foundation for coordination of policy toward North Korea. Both U.S. president Barack Obama and South Korean president Lee Myung-bak have agreed that their top policy objective vis-à-vis North Korea is its complete denuclearization. Their common goal is to promote a regional strategy that constrains North Korea's destabilizing activities and counters the risks resulting from its nuclear and missile activities. In the wake of the ship sinking, the two administrations have worked particularly closely to forge bilateral and multilateral responses designed to strengthen deterrence and ensure that North Korea cannot engage in such provocations with impunity.

Productive Sino-U.S. consultations on North Korea have been lauded in recent years as evidence that the United States and China can work together to address common security challenges. Conversely, the failure to collaborate to achieve North Korea's denuclearization will represent a setback and an obstacle to other areas of U.S.-China security cooperation. For this reason, it is essential for the United States and China to develop a clear understanding regarding how to deal with North Korea, thereby establishing a framework for lasting stability on a nonnuclear Korean peninsula and in Northeast Asia.

There is widespread pessimism that North Korea will voluntarily give up its nuclear capabilities through negotiations alone, and China,

Japan, and South Korea are reluctant to pursue tougher, coercive steps due to fears of instability. The rollback of North Korea's nuclear program will not be easy, especially given that no state that has conducted a nuclear test has subsequently reversed course without a change in political leadership. The Task Force notes, however, that despite the difficulty of the challenge, the danger posed by North Korea is sufficiently severe, and the costs of inaction and acquiescence so high, that the United States and its partners must continue to press for denuclearization.

Although the six-party process remains the preferred framework, the United States and its partners may in the end find it necessary to apply nondiplomatic tools such as sanctions or even military measures, especially if North Korea conducts further nuclear or long-range missile tests or proliferates nuclear materials or technologies to other states or to nonstate actors. Specifically, the Task Force calls for the establishment of a dialogue with China about the future of the Korean peninsula, for bilateral talks with North Korea regarding missile development, and for the continuation of close consultations with allies South Korea and Japan.

The Task Force finds that the Obama administration should deal with North Korea's policy challenges in the following order: prevent nuclear exports to others (horizontal proliferation), stop further development of North Korea nuclear capability (vertical proliferation), roll back Korea's nuclear program, plan for potential North Korean instability, integrate North Korea into the international community, and help the people of North Korea.

The report takes stock of the North Korean threat and the Obama administration's responses thus far, and considers the four major policy courses available to the United States. It then explores the motivations and interests of the other parties in the Six Party Talks and underscores the importance of a regional approach anchored by U.S.-South Korea cooperation and by Chinese action. The report then looks beyond the nuclear problem to take account of important items on the agenda with North Korea and the valuable bilateral relationship with South Korea.

The North Korean Challenge

North Korea's series of provocations in the first half of 2009—including missile and nuclear tests—defied an emerging Northeast Asian regional consensus on denuclearization of the Korean peninsula, suspended the normalization of diplomatic relations between parties in the region, and deferred the pursuit of economic development and peace on the peninsula and in Northeast Asia. These provocations underscored the failure of two decades of U.S. and international diplomatic efforts to block North Korea's nuclear development, as well as North Korea's seeming imperviousness to international pressure and sanctions.

Past U.S. administrations have attempted bilateral deal-making and multilateral implementation (the Clinton administration's Agreed Framework), neglect (first George W. Bush administration, 2001–2004), and bilateral engagement within the context of Six Party Talks (second George W. Bush administration, 2005–2008). None of these approaches was successful in deterring North Korea from pursuit of its nuclear program. Five previous CFR-sponsored Independent Task Force reports have documented the persistent challenge represented by North Korea and the deficiencies of the international responses.[2]

North Korea conducted its first nuclear test in 2006. This and its subsequent test constitute a direct challenge to peace and stability in Northeast Asia. The risk of proliferation of fissile materials to other regions has ramifications for stability in the Middle East, as well as for the global nonproliferation regime. North Korea's nuclear tests sharpen the dilemma for the international community over whether it is willing to use coercive tools—such as pressing for tougher sanctions under new UN resolutions targeting North Korean trade and financial transactions, implementing a more intrusive export control regime, or additional military measures—in combination with negotiations in an effort to roll back North Korea's nuclear program.

President Obama inherited this perilous situation when he took office in 2009, following last-ditch efforts on the part of the George W. Bush administration to convince the Democratic People's Republic of Korea (DPRK) to accept international verification of its nuclear facilities as part of a February 2007 implementing agreement under the six-party framework. Rather than taking conciliatory measures to open the way for a new relationship with the Obama administration in early 2009, North Korea appears to have placed every possible obstacle in the way of renewed dialogue. In the process, North Korea undertook a series of actions aimed at pushing the Obama administration toward implicit recognition, if not explicit acceptance, of it as a nuclear weapons state.

Before Obama's inauguration, the DPRK Foreign Ministry asserted that there was no linkage between normalization of U.S.-DPRK diplomatic relations and North Korea's denuclearization, instead asserting that North Korea would maintain a nuclear deterrent "as long as it is exposed even to the slightest U.S. nuclear threat."[3] Then, on April 5, 2009, North Korea launched a rocket that could be used for long-range missiles, claiming that it had the right to pursue a peaceful satellite launch. This action was immediately condemned by Obama in a speech in Prague the next day on the need for global nuclear arms reductions. President Obama criticized North Korea's actions, saying, "Rules must be binding. Violations must be punished. Words must mean something."[4] The Obama administration pursued a UN presidential statement condemning the launch as a violation of UN Security Council (UNSC) Resolution 1718, which imposed restrictions on North Korean missile launch capacities following the DPRK's 2006 nuclear test.[5] North Korea responded with outrage to this condemnation, pledging to walk away from the Six Party Talks and threatening to conduct a second nuclear test, which it did on May 25, 2009.[6]

In response to this test, the Obama administration worked energetically at the UN to gain unanimous support for UNSC Resolution 1874. The resolution, passed in June 2009, calls on member states to exercise strengthened vigilance against North Korean horizontal proliferation activities—that is, the exchange of North Korean nuclear-related technology and materials with other state or nonstate actors.[7] Through the end of 2009, the resolution had been successful in blocking a half-dozen North Korean shipments of weapons and other suspicious goods under the UN sanctions.[8] The Obama administration also appointed a sanctions coordinator to promote international implementation of the resolution. However, such counterproliferation activities will not be sufficient to completely stop the illicit spread of nuclear technology and know-how to new nuclear aspirants.

Beyond implementing sanctions imposed under UNSC Resolution 1874, the Obama administration has not attempted to draw red lines around North Korean activities that would provoke a stronger U.S. response. North Korea has crossed every previous line the United States has drawn, including around the testing of a nuclear device, with impunity.[9] Following North Korea's 2006 nuclear test, President Bush attempted to draw yet another line around North Korean proliferation, but that did not stop covert North Korean collaboration with Syria on construction of a nuclear plant to produce plutonium, a plant that was bombed by Israel in September 2007. The only red line that remains is the threat (reinforced indirectly by the conclusions of the April 2010 Nuclear Posture Review) that as long as North Korea is outside the Nuclear Nonproliferation Treaty (NPT) it will be treated as the prime suspect and be the target of immediate retaliation by the United States in the event of an act of nonstate nuclear terrorism.[10] In light of past U.S. failures to enforce its red lines with North Korea, the challenge for the Obama administration is how to take actions that would enhance the credibility of U.S. threats.

CURRENT U.S. POLICY

Early in his term, President Obama declared that his administration would "not fall into the same pattern [as previous administrations] with North Korea." Rather, he said, it is "incumbent upon all of us to insist that nations like Iran and North Korea do not game the system.... Those who seek peace cannot stand idly by as nations arm themselves for nuclear war."[11] Defense Secretary Robert M. Gates stated that the Obama administration "will not buy this horse for a third time."[12] Secretary of State Hillary Clinton said, "The international community failed to prevent North Korea from developing nuclear weapons. We are now engaged in diplomatic efforts to roll back this development."[13] These statements, coupled with past negotiating experience, highlight the deep levels of mistrust U.S. policymakers harbor toward North

Korea. The dominant American perception of this experience is that North Korea pursues negotiations primarily to extract concessions from its counterparts while making commitments it does not intend to keep.

While enforcing sanctions, the Obama administration has continued to exert what it calls strategic patience and extend an open diplomatic hand to North Korea, contingent on North Korea's return to the six-party framework and the path of denuclearization. Following Special Representative Stephen W. Bosworth's December 2009 meetings in Pyongyang, Secretary Clinton stated that "the approach that our administration is taking is of strategic patience in close coordination with our six-party allies."[14] This is characteristic of the current U.S. policy approach: a continued commitment to denuclearization, dedication to the six-party process, willingness to engage (with conditions), and efforts to work within multilateral frameworks to sanction and pressure North Korea.

Meanwhile, North Korea's efforts to develop its missile programs continue unchecked.[15] The Pentagon's February 2010 Ballistic Missile Defense Review report concluded that if North Korea's nuclear and missile programs continue to progress along the current trajectory, North Korea will eventually have both a nuclear capability and the capacity to deliver a nuclear weapon to its neighbors and to the United States.[16] The task of addressing North Korea's nuclear status is much harder now that North Korea has conducted two nuclear tests. The challenges posed will likewise be even more difficult once the country develops an effective nuclear weapons delivery capability.

Despite accepting the six-party framework established by the George W. Bush administration as the main vehicle for pursuing negotiations, the Obama administration has signaled a shift from past policy by emphasizing reassurance of South Korean and Japanese allies. This is partly a response to the perception in the region that the George W. Bush administration leaned too heavily on bilateral negotiations with North Korea at the expense of alliance consultation. Special Representative Bosworth has engaged in frequent policy consultations with North Korea's neighbors, including China and Russia, to promote regional cohesion in response to North Korea's nuclear pursuits. When North Korea initiated a "charm offensive" in the latter part of 2009 by renewing diplomatic outreach to the United States and South Korea, the Obama administration responded by sending Bosworth to

Pyongyang in December 2009 to convey the message that North Korea should return to the denuclearization path by coming back to the Six Party Talks.

The Task Force finds that the Obama administration has employed primarily reactive measures in response to North Korean provocations. Secretary Clinton described the baseline for U.S. policy when she stated that "within the framework of the Six Party Talks, we are prepared to meet bilaterally with North Korea, but North Korea's return to the negotiating table is not enough. Current sanctions will not be relaxed until Pyongyang takes verifiable, irreversible steps toward complete denuclearization. Its leaders should be under no illusion that the United States will ever have normal, sanctions-free relations with a nuclear armed North Korea."[17]

Despite the strong words, the Obama administration's actions to date suggest that the objective of rollback of North Korea's nuclear program is halfhearted. The time frame for achieving denuclearization is so vague that there is a significant risk that "strategic patience" will result in acquiescence to North Korea's nuclear status as a fait accompli. Responsibility within the administration for implementation of policy toward North Korea has been divided under several envoys into different baskets—negotiations, sanctions implementation, and human rights—with no clear evidence that these discrete missions are backed by a sense of urgency or priority at senior levels in the administration. The Task Force finds that the Obama administration's current approach does not go far enough in developing a strategy to counter North Korea's continuing nuclear development or potential for proliferation.

U.S. Policy Options

Although the facts of North Korea's progress in pursuing nuclear weapons are undeniable, how neighboring states and the United States respond to North Korea's nuclear ambitions will have significant regional and global political and security consequences. By testing two nuclear devices, the DPRK has challenged the United States and the region to accept its nuclear status. Ironically, although intended as a declaration of strength, North Korea's nuclear and missile tests also show its weakness, vulnerability, and desperation, underscoring its political isolation, failing economy, lagging conventional military capabilities, and keen desire for international acceptance and recognition. It is this reality that may allow a coordinated response to succeed.

The Task Force debated four policy options for the United States and its partners: (1) explicit acquiescence, (2) containment and management, (3) rollback, and (4) regime change. The Task Force concedes that U.S. policy is constrained and that the United States has limited ability to effect change on its own. Given the reality of a bad situation with few good choices, the Task Force considered the pros and cons of each option and its likelihood of adoption and success. The Task Force ultimately rejects options 1 and 4, acknowledges the interim benefits of option 2, and endorses option 3—denuclearization.

OPTION 1—ACQUIESCENCE

The first option is that the Obama administration could conclude that there are no viable options for achieving North Korea's denuclearization, thus conceding failure and acquiescing to its nuclear status. In this case, the administration might accept the idea put forward by the North Korean leadership that an improved diplomatic relationship should be delinked from the denuclearization decision by focusing on reducing tensions and improving relations with North Korea regardless of its nuclear status. Such an approach would immediately ease the crisis in relations with North Korea and open a much broader array of diplomatic and political options for bilateral engagement.

Explicit acquiescence, however, would threaten the sustainability of existing U.S. alliances in Asia. Japan and South Korea would consider U.S. acquiescence as undermining Washington's ability to provide for their security, regardless of U.S. security commitments of extended deterrence and provision of a nuclear umbrella as protection. Explicit acceptance of a nuclear North Korea might also catalyze consideration of a wider range of military options in South Korea and Japan, including the acquisition of preemptive strike capabilities and nuclear weapons in an attempt to restore a regional balance in capabilities, thus setting off a regional arms race. Moreover, the people of Japan and South Korea would not accept a nuclear North Korea, and U.S. political opposition would likely make political hay out of the issue, accusing the Obama administration of appeasement. Acquiescence would be an embarrassing admission of defeat and would weaken perceptions of U.S. power around the world. Such capitulation would make negotiations with Iran and other nuclear hopefuls more difficult, if not impossible.

Current U.S. policy acknowledges the de facto reality that North Korea has developed a nuclear capacity, but does not accept North Korea as a nuclear weapons state. This lack of acceptance will be credible only if the United States continues to take commensurate efforts to roll back North Korea's nuclear program. Benign neglect, or the absence of such efforts, would amount to acceptance of a nuclear North Korea.

The Task Force finds that any U.S. administration is unlikely to openly acquiesce to North Korean nuclear ambitions and that the negative consequences for the nuclear nonproliferation regime outweigh any potential benefits of this course. Such acquiescence would weaken credibility of U.S. security commitments in the region, and North Korea would stand as a monument to the failure of the NPT and as a model for other potential nuclear aspirants.

OPTION 2—MANAGE AND CONTAIN

A second option is to pursue a policy that classifies the North Korean nuclear challenge as a problem to be managed, with a low likelihood of near-term resolution. Recognizing that it will take a long time and a concerted effort to denuclearize North Korea, the administration would work in concert with partners to contain North Korean onward proliferation as its primary objective, while blocking North Korean vertical proliferation by preventing it, through a combination of negotiations and coercive measures, from increasing the size or the sophistication of its nuclear arsenal and missile delivery capacity. The Task Force believes that this approach—containing the problem and managing the reality while paying lip service to the objective of rollback—is the closest among the four options to the Obama administration's current policy.

Conditional on support from allies Japan and South Korea, efforts to prevent North Korea's vertical proliferation could include a U.S. strike on North Korea's long-range missile launch facilities (akin to recommendations made by Ashton B. Carter and William J. Perry before North Korea's 2006 long-range missile launch) in the event that North Korea prepares once again to defy existing UNSC resolutions. Prior to North Korea's two nuclear tests, this recommendation seemed premature and dangerous, but cannot be ruled out easily now that an enhanced missile capacity would give North Korea the capacity to deliver a nuclear weapon.[18]

A "manage and contain" approach focuses on risk reduction first, while waiting for circumstances conducive to North Korea's eventual denuclearization. It prioritizes "three *nos*" as primary immediate objectives in dealing with North Korea: no export of nuclear technologies, no more bombs, and no "better" bombs.[19] The Obama administration would pursue counterproliferation aggressively through implementation of UN resolutions while taking steps to constrain North Korea from building more bombs by negotiating a missile moratorium or improving its existing arsenal through additional nuclear tests by ensuring that the scope of international sanctions is expanded in retaliation for further tests. To back these counterproliferation efforts, the administration should clearly state that as long as North Korea remains outside of the NPT and uncommitted to denuclearization, it is suspect number one in the event of nuclear terrorism by non-state actors, thereby putting North Korea in the crosshairs for a U.S. retaliatory strike if such an event were to occur.

This approach would focus on maintaining a freeze on nuclear development activities at the Yongbyon facility and on building international support to urge North Korea against conducting any further nuclear tests. Another facet of this approach would address North Korea's vertical proliferation—that is, North Korean efforts to mount a nuclear device on a missile—by attempting to negotiate a moratorium on North Korean missile tests.

Even if the United States remains adamantly opposed to North Korea's continued development of a nuclear weapons and delivery capability, there are limits to what it can do without cooperation from North Korea's neighbors, especially China. China shares the objective of containing North Korea's program and preventing North Korean actions that would further heighten tensions but is unlikely to pursue the potentially destabilizing path that might result from pressing for denuclearization of North Korea. By pursuing the option of simply managing and containing North Korea's nuclear program, perhaps in the hope that North Korea's own internal politics might eventually dictate abandonment of nuclear weapons, the United States would avoid a quarrel with China, given China's prioritization of regional stability over denuclearization.

The Task Force concedes that containment is attractive and probably the easiest and most practical option, given the difficulty of achieving rollback and the undesirability of escalating a sense of crisis on the Korean peninsula when the Obama administration is facing so many other challenges. Both China and South Korea, given the choice between facing a new crisis or deferring such a crisis in favor of the short-term maintenance of the status quo, may believe that the status quo serves their interests, especially if they are able to work together to contain the negative spillover effects of North Korea's nuclear ambitions. However, such an approach will not resolve the problem, and manage and contain must be seen only as an interim option.

The Task Force finds that though containment is essential to U.S. counterproliferation objectives, such a strategy by itself is insufficient. It risks the likelihood that, over time, the overall security situation will deteriorate as North Korea continues to secretly make progress in its missile development and nascent nuclear capability. The manage and contain approach may also lead to the perception that the United States is interested only in counterproliferation, leading eventually to acquiescence rather than denuclearization, regardless of administration assertions to the contrary. The Task Force considers that manage and contain, as evidenced by the current approach, may be a useful interim strategy, but does not resolve the larger problem and must ultimately be coupled with continued efforts to denuclearize. Implementation of this option is necessary, but not enough to achieve denuclearization, which remains an important U.S. objective.

OPTION 3—ROLLBACK

A third option would be to immediately and consistently press for North Korea's return to the path of denuclearization. This approach would involve a stepped-up combination of sanctions and incentives designed to make North Korea abandon its nuclear programs. There would be constant political pressure by the international community on North Korea—including the ratcheting up of the international sanctions regime—to limit its alternatives to negotiation. In return for cooperation, North Korea would receive political and economic benefits, such as development and energy assistance, through implementation of the September 2005 Six Party Joint Statement. Conversely, its failure to cooperate would result in enforced sanctions and other penalties.

This option envisions a definitive resolution of North Korea's nuclear challenge by strengthened regional security cooperation between the United States and North Korea's neighbors. It means that the Obama administration must treat the rollback of North Korea's nuclear program as a realizable objective, and use all the tools at its disposal (including raising the profile of the work of the sanctions coordinator) to increase pressure on North Korea, both directly and indirectly, by coordinating with other members of the six-party framework. Such an approach requires that the United States convince China that denuclearization is necessary for long-term regional stability and find ways to encourage China to cooperate. Active efforts to roll back North Korea's nuclear gains run the risk of heightening tensions on the Korean peninsula in the short term, but these temporary pressures would be relieved by North Korea's resumption of the implementation of its denuclearization commitments outlined in the Six Party Joint Statement.

Pursuit of this option entails North Korea's neighbors working in concert with one another to implement agreed-on UN sanctions until North Korea recommits itself to denuclearization. Any party, such as China, that fails to fully implement its obligation under the UN resolutions would be effectively validating North Korea's claim to be a nuclear weapons state. Thus, it should not be in the interest of any party to prematurely relent until North Korea's leadership takes actions in the direction of denuclearization.

If North Korea returns to the Six Party Talks and resumes implementation of its denuclearization commitments, the other parties would have to also meet their own obligations under the agreement. North Korean officials complained that the other parties were dragging their feet in providing the economic assistance promised under the implementing agreement of February 13, 2007, thereby providing a pretext for North Korea to avoid its own obligations. The United States and Japan have obligations under the joint statement to normalize political relations with North Korea, including eventual diplomatic recognition and the exchange of diplomatic representation. The joint statement also references the need for a separate negotiating forum to establish arrangements to replace the existing armistice with a permanent peace mechanism.

North Korean leaders must be convinced by mobilized coercive measures preventing such an outcome that the pursuit of nuclear weapons is hazardous to their regime survival, and that a path toward denuclearization would provide them new opportunities in the form of available expanded political and economic benefits. North Korea's leadership has spent decades pursuing nuclear weapons as the silver bullet to assure sovereignty, respect, and deterrence of external powers. It is unlikely to voluntarily give up this pursuit without a combination of political and economic inducements, which may come in the form of energy and economic development assistance. For this reason, it will be essential for the U.S. administration to outline concrete benefits that North Korea would gain from denuclearization. South Korean president Lee Myung-bak has proposed a massive development commitment to North Korea if it abandons its nuclear weapons and opens to the outside world. But North Korean leaders would be more likely to view such a proposal as credible if the United States also offered to develop a new relationship with the North.

The Task Force believes that the regional consensus must be pushed from rhetoric to action and that the strength of China's commitments to support and enforce global nonproliferation should be tested. Thus the Task Force believes option 3—continued pressure on North Korea to return to the Six Party Talks and to a path of denuclearization—is the necessary course of action.

OPTION 4—REGIME CHANGE

A fourth option for achieving denuclearization would be to pursue regime change in North Korea. This might include support for subversive activities intended to undermine the current leadership, expansion of economic sanctions, strengthened measures to inspect and interdict all cargo to and from North Korea, and a rhetorical policy designed to publicly support regime change.

Given the widespread pessimism regarding the likelihood of the current regime voluntarily giving up its nuclear weapons, its lack of credibility in implementing past diplomatic agreements, and its willingness to sell conventional weapons and missile technologies to the highest bidder, this approach prioritizes denuclearization over stability. It assumes that any negotiations will be a pretext for delay rather than a vehicle for successfully managing or resolving the dangers posed by North Korea's nuclear weapons program.

It also implicitly assumes that a new North Korean regime would be more amenable to negotiations and willing to give up the weapons, though this may not be the case. Given current North Korean leader Kim Jong-il's advanced age and reported ill health, leadership may pass to a designated successor, who may or may not continue the policies of the current regime. There are many uncertainties and dangers in a regime change scenario (detailed in a later section on contingency planning), but the option accepts North Korea's destabilization as a means to ensure denuclearization. This option entails a willingness to bear the immediate costs of instability for the establishment of a new order in North Korea, either through Korean reunification or the installation of a reform-oriented North Korean leadership.

An obstacle to the regime change option is that it contradicts the high priority North Korea's neighbors place on a stable transition to a new leadership in North Korea. As a result, U.S.-driven regime change would come at a high cost to U.S. interests and relationships in the region. China prioritizes regional peace and stability over denuclearization as a policy objective. The South Korean government has also traditionally been cautious about pursuing externally imposed regime change on the North for fear that the near-term costs of a sudden transition in the North would be more than the South is willing or able to bear. The fears of violence, flows of refugees, spillover, and costs are not unreasonable or unfounded, and the United States should take those concerns into consideration.

Nonetheless, the option of actively supporting regime change should be held in reserve as a possible course of action in the event that North Korea continues to pursue horizontal or vertical proliferation or nuclear development activities in defiance of existing UN resolutions. North Korea's failure to return to the path of denuclearization could also lead the United States and other members of the Six Party Talks to conclude that regime change is the only possible way to roll back North Korea's nuclear program.

It is unlikely that the Obama administration will pursue this option, at least not openly, given its stated commitment to engagement and international norms. It should be noted, however, that several Task Force members thought that this course should be quietly considered in parallel to a public commitment of continued pressure to denuclearize.

NORTH KOREA'S INTEGRATION WITH THE OUTSIDE WORLD

To counter North Korea's provocations, the United States has historically emphasized the employment of sanctions against North Korea to isolate it from the international community. However, by reinforcing its isolation, continuation of a comprehensive sanctions regime against North Korea may ironically strengthen the regime's capacity to maintain political control. For this reason, the Obama administration should consider an array of engagement initiatives along with the UN sanctions that have been targeted at North Korea's nuclear and missile programs.

Expanding the exposure of individual North Koreans to the outside world may eventually result in internally driven regime transformation, a result that the United States and North Korea's neighbors would welcome and support. Engagement may also lead to a greater understanding of North Korea's infamously opaque decision-making processes and increase levels of trust in the region, while constraining North Korea from pursuing rash actions.

Engagement strategies, including support for more liberalized visa policies, nongovernmental, educational, and cultural exchanges, and other methods of engagement, should be designed to lay the foundations for political change by providing North Koreans with more exposure to international norms and standards.[20] The main criterion by which the United States should judge engagement strategies toward North Korea is whether they will increase the pace of change in North Korea or can be used to strengthen the political control of the regime.

The economic lever has proved a politically powerful tool for promoting reform-oriented political leadership in other inward-focused societies, and a U.S. policy of selective engagement with North Korea may help facilitate government-led economic reforms. Engagement could facilitate grassroots-led marketization and the spread of capitalism, which ultimately could undermine the North Korean leadership's efforts to maintain strict economic and political controls over its population. The development of economic ties with outside partners could also fuel a domestic political competition between political reformers and conservatives. The small-scale spread of farmers' markets and slow but steady dissemination of information across North Korea's borders already challenge the North Korean leadership's ability to completely control the population.[21]

North Korea's economic transformation and integration into the global community would be a bigger threat to its own leadership than to the international community. For example, North Korea has to meet international standards on reporting and transparency regarding its internal financial system to receive loans from international financial institutions (IFIs). Its efforts to meet IFI reporting and transparency requirements are an important vehicle in achieving mutually beneficial integration with the international financial community.[22]

The Obama administration—in close coordination with South Korea—should pursue forms of engagement with North Korea most likely to improve the lot of North Koreans and bring about change in the country, regardless of the policies of the North Korean leadership. While implementing sanctions targeted primarily at North Korea's nuclear and missile programs, the administration should support nongovernmental exchanges in areas where grassroots or nongovernmental interaction might broaden North Korea's exposure to international norms.

A Regional Framework for Stability

Each member of the Six Party Talks—the United States, China, Japan, Russia, and South Korea—has its own set of interests, political priorities, and domestic constraints and pressures regarding North Korea. Despite having divergent views, all have agreed to the Six Party Joint Statement—supporting denuclearization, the normalization of relations, and advancement of peace and prosperity on the Korean peninsula—and signed on to sanctions resolutions. Any hope of resolving the North Korean standoff will depend on all parties cooperating with one another and being firm with North Korea. China in particular has a central role to play.

CHINA'S KOREA POLICY AND KOREA'S ROLE IN U.S.-CHINA RELATIONS

The Task Force finds that China's policy toward the Korean peninsula—and the role of cooperation and competition on Korean issues as a component of the U.S.-China relationship—is a critical variable that influences the range of available tools for addressing North Korea's nuclear program. The current DPRK regime's survival depends on China's willingness to supply the necessary food and fuel to ensure North Korean sustainability. If North Korea's economy is on life support, the Chinese are providing the necessities to keep it alive.

Although China and North Korea have a shared history and ideological foundation, bilateral ties have frayed over the past two decades as China has taken a path of economic reform and North Korea has continued to pursue autarchy and isolation. Hence, China and North Korea have less and less in common. In fact, China's policy toward North Korea is contradictory to overall trends in People's Republic of China (PRC) foreign policy. Whereas China works to promote regional stability, a nuclear North Korea provides a fundamental challenge to security in the region. These contradictions are at the core of China's policy dilemma as it manages its relations with North Korea.[23]

That China continues to view the Korean peninsula through the lens of its relationship with the United States exacerbates these contradictions. China has continuously insisted that the core motivation for North Korea's nuclear pursuits lies in its mistrust of the United States and that security assurances in the context of improvements in the U.S.-DPRK political relationship would belie North Korea's need for a nuclear program. Even though North Korea's nuclear pursuits have directly challenged Chinese interests, mistrust of U.S. intentions on the Korean peninsula—which dates to the Korean War—has inhibited Sino-U.S. cooperation on Korean issues.

China has emerged as a mediator between Washington and Pyongyang by hosting the Six Party Talks, a role in which Chinese diplomats have taken great pride, but Chinese mediation efforts are more focused on China's desire to keep both sides calm rather than on achieving a solution. North Korea's continued insistence on defying Chinese efforts to mediate—even as its economy depends utterly on Chinese imports—demonstrates China's patience.

While China is concerned about North Korea's development of a nuclear weapons capacity, its greater concern is the possibility of North Korean instability. For this reason, China emphasizes negotiations and has been reluctant to consider coercive measures as part of its strategy toward North Korea. China remains wary of U.S. preferred tools for addressing the North Korean nuclear issue, eschewing pressure and sanctions in favor of economic incentives and attempts to entice North Korea to join in dialogue and cooperation. A U.S. approach that emphasizes regional cohesion in dealing with North Korea requires Chinese cooperation, but there are limits to the range of options China is willing to consider.

China wants to maintain its own independent approach to the Korean peninsula, even as it cooperates with the United States. Following North Korea's first nuclear test in 2006, some Chinese analysts criticized their government for working too closely with the United States, which, they charged, resulted in a cooling of Sino-North Korean ties and a perceived loss of Chinese influence in North Korea. After North Korea's 2009 test, Beijing chose to reinforce ties with Pyongyang even while going along with a strong UNSC resolution condemning the test.

This bifurcated course of action may have preserved Chinese influence in North Korea, but China has thus far been unable to use that influence to convince North Korea to recommit itself to denuclearization.

The task of persuading China to assume greater responsibility for North Korea's denuclearization is a challenging one. China's leaders must come to the conclusion that a nuclear North Korea under its current unpredictable leadership risks the stability that China has invested so heavily in trying to preserve. Past experience suggests that China takes action only when it perceives increased tensions or the possibility of military conflict between North Korea and the United States. In early 2003, China determined that it would play a more active mediating role when it appeared that the prospect of military confrontation between the United States and North Korea was rising. China has also been concerned about the negative effect of North Korean provocation of its neighbors. For example, Chinese leaders were alarmed when North Korea's 2006 tests prompted discussions in Japan about preemption and the question of whether to consider its own nuclear option.[24]

China has also responded when its leaders perceive that North Korea is a high priority for the United States or feel that the United States might negotiate directly with North Korea. President Bush's personal efforts to discuss North Korea with Chinese president Hu Jintao mobilized enhanced Sino-U.S. cooperation, though former assistant secretary of state Christopher R. Hill's visit to North Korea in June 2007 without consulting with or debriefing Beijing evoked concern.[25] For China and the United States to succeed in coordinating their policies toward North Korea, the subject of how to achieve a nonnuclear Korean peninsula will have to be treated as a top priority on the bilateral agenda, ideally at the presidential level.

It will not be easy for the United States to catalyze further cooperation from China. But Chinese leaders should seriously consider the possibility that North Korean proliferation resulting in nuclear terrorism would likely draw a much sharper U.S. military response.

China worries about the emergence of an unfriendly regime in a future unified Korea. If the Obama administration's efforts to build regional cohesion and closer Sino-U.S. cooperation are to bear fruit, the United States will need to clarify its objectives toward the Korean peninsula and provide reassurance about its intentions. The Task Force calls for a dialogue with China about the future of the Korean peninsula and "principles" of a united Korea. Such a dialogue could include discussion about the process of potential unification and what a unified Korea might look like, including the number, location, and even presence of U.S. troops in Korea and a pledge to keep the peninsula nuclear-free. Any discussion with China regarding desired outcomes or future developments on the Korean peninsula would have to be based on full, prior U.S. coordination with allies in Seoul and Tokyo.

U.S.-JAPAN ALLIANCE AND KOREAN PENINSULA

The emergence of a new government in Japan under the Democratic Party of Japan (DPJ) in September 2009 is a historic development following more than five decades of rule by the Liberal Democratic Party. This development by itself may not shift Japan's policy toward North Korea in the near term, but recent friction and uncertainty in the U.S.-Japan alliance (in part over disagreement on the relocation of the U.S. air base at Futenma to another site) could become a new variable in the overall international approach to the North Korean nuclear problem. Although there appears to be little likelihood that Japan would take independent initiatives toward North Korea before its summer 2010 Upper House election, a DPJ-led government might eventually consider the possibility of pursuing renewed bilateral diplomacy with North Korea.

Japan faces near-term and long-term challenges in its relations with North Korea. The near-term challenge has two aspects. The first is related to the Japanese public's strong expectation that its government will focus on the accounting for missing Japanese citizens abducted or presumed abducted by North Korea. This issue involves a number of Japanese citizens kidnapped by North Koreans from Japanese soil (and perhaps from abroad) in the 1970s and 1980s whose whereabouts have not been satisfactorily investigated. To Japan, the U.S. position appears to be too narrowly focused on a denuclearization-for-normalization deal. Critics in Japan say that the United States has failed to take into account the fervent Japanese desire to see progress on the abduction issue. Without North Korean cooperation on this issue, substantive Japanese assistance, as part of any denuclearization agreement, will prove difficult. To the extent that Japanese politicians and the Japanese public continue to make the abduction issue Japan's foremost priority, Japan is unlikely to contribute effectively to diplomatic efforts focused on denuclearization through the Six Party Talks.

A second aspect of Japan's near-term challenge is Japanese expectations and anxieties over whether the United States can be depended on to defend it from North Korean aggression. These anxieties were compounded by the U.S. decision during the George W. Bush administration to reengage in the Six Party Talks after initially taking a hard-line position against North Korea's nuclear and illicit activities. This change in approach was seen in Japan as an about-face. The Bush administration's October 2008 decision to take North Korea off the terrorist list in return for its incomplete declaration of its nuclear facilities was particularly damaging to U.S.-Japan relations. The 1998 North Korean Taepodong test and North Korea's 2006 missile test also reminded the Japanese public that North Korea's missile delivery systems pose a direct threat to nearby Japan, yet missiles are not yet publicly on the U.S. diplomatic agenda or the agenda of the Six Party Talks. Thus, Japanese concerns about the reliability of U.S. security guarantees and North Korea's missile program cause Japan to be suspicious of any U.S. efforts to negotiate directly with North Korea about its nuclear weapons program.

The longer-term dilemma relates to Japanese concerns about what a future unified Korea might look like. Japan and Korea have a complicated historical relationship, and Japan worries that Korean reunification might alter the status quo on the Korean peninsula in ways that could be detrimental to Japan. If a unified Korea is hostile to Japan, it would fuel long-standing Japanese security concerns. Japanese uncertainty about the future orientation of the Korean peninsula affects its role in the six-party process and causes it to be cautious rather than assertive.

The United States should continue to reassure Japan that progress on denuclearization will not come at the expense of Japan's concerns about abductees, and at the same time make clear to North Korea that it cannot neglect the abductee issue in talks with Japan. The United States should coordinate closely with Japan on any future missile negotiations with North Korea while continuing to strengthen missile defense capabilities against the North Korean threat.

RUSSIA AND THE KOREAN PENINSULA

Russia has historically played a role on the Korean peninsula, but its capacity to influence the security situation there is low. Its participation in the Six Party Talks affirms Russia's relevance and role in Northeast Asian affairs despite its current relative lack of regional influence. Russia supports the denuclearization of the Korean peninsula and welcomes progress toward inter-Korean reconciliation and possible unification, but has relatively few diplomatic or other resources available to contribute to the process. As a result, Russia's sway in diplomatic efforts to achieve North Korea's denuclearization has been marginal.

Nonetheless, Russia maintains a long-term geostrategic interest in Korean stability. Russian security concerns would arise only in the event of a single great power assuming a dominant role on the peninsula. Russia would welcome a unified Korea that is friendly or neutral and would oppose the continuation of a U.S. military presence in a unified Korea. But Korean reunification is unlikely to have a direct effect on Russia's vital security interests.[26]

The Task Force finds that the North Korea challenge is one in which the United States and Russia have overlapping concerns and no great difference of view. The Task Force further notes that the Six Party Talks provide a forum for positive and constructive U.S.-Russia cooperation and coordination, which helps to build trust and foster ties that may be useful in other areas, such as Iran. Vice President Joseph R. Biden Jr., for example, has credited Strategic Arms Reduction Treaty (START) negotiations with Russia for strengthening "the global consensus that nations who violate their NPT obligations should be held to account."[27]

Moreover, as a member of the UN Security Council, a nuclear weapons state, and a longtime participant in nuclear arms and cooperative threat reduction activities, Russia may have important skills and technical expertise to contribute in practical terms to North Korea's denuclearization process. For example, Moscow has shown interest in developing railway and energy links in the region that could provide North Korea with economic development benefits in the context of denuclearization. Although its role and interest in the forum has been relatively passive, Russia values its participation in the Six Party Talks and has the potential to make technical contributions if North Korea moves to denuclearize.

The new START treaty, signed by presidents Obama and Dmitry Medvedev in April 2010, provides a strategic context for cooperation to address North Korea as a state that violated NPT obligations and withdrew from the treaty. Obama administration statements imply that renewed U.S.-Russia steps toward disarmament should be accompanied by commensurate responsibilities among nonnuclear states to uphold commitments to denuclearization, including application of pressure against North Korea and Iran as challengers to the treaty. The United States should deepen diplomatic coordination with Russia regarding policy toward North Korea and encourage Russia's continued involvement in and tangible contributions to multilateral efforts to denuclearize North Korea.

U.S.-SOUTH KOREA ALLIANCE

Inter-Korean relations deteriorated rapidly with the February 2008 inauguration of Lee Myung-bak as president of South Korea, whose more skeptical approach to North Korea overturned a decade of progressive efforts to engage the North and promote peaceful coexistence. North Korea responded with numerous aggressive statements and threats of attack, although its conventional military capabilities lag far behind the South.

The divergence of priorities between the United States and South Korea on policy toward North Korea has been a continuing challenge for the U.S.-South Korea alliance since the negotiation of the Agreed Framework in the early 1990s. The Republic of Korea's (ROK) priorities have understandably been focused on the peninsula, favoring stability and engagement, while the United States has larger global concerns about proliferation and ramifications beyond the peninsula. Ongoing consultations are needed to bridge this gap in perspectives, which results from the U.S. view about the dangers of North Korean proliferation potential compared with South Korea's prioritization of the need for peninsular stability.

With the exception of a short period during the Clinton and Kim Dae-jung administrations in 1999–2000, when both the United States and South Korea were pursuing active engagement with North Korea, the management of differences between Washington and Seoul in their approaches to North Korea has required frequent attention. Alliance coordination on North Korea became a major source of difficulty during the Bush and Roh administrations and even limited military planning for North Korean contingencies.

These differences in priorities, however, have been minimized as a result of Lee Myung-bak's strong commitment to North Korea's denuclearization and the breakdown of the Six Party Talks in late 2008. This commitment was reflected during South Korea's 2007 presidential election campaign, when Lee announced his "Denuclearization, Openness, 3,000" policy. As Lee reiterated in his inaugural address, he committed to make South Korean investments in North Korea with the objective of raising North Korea's per capita GDP to $3,000. These investments would be conditioned on North Korea pursuing policies of denuclearization and openness to the outside world.[28]

The Lee administration came into office in February 2008 determined to restore U.S.-ROK alliance coordination toward North Korea, effectively aligning its priority of denuclearization with that of the United States. Although this emphasis has caused tensions in inter-Korea relations, the Lee administration's approach improved relations between the United States and South Korea at the end of the Bush administration and under the Obama administration. It also deprives North Korea of the leverage with which it had previously exploited differences between Washington and Seoul. The Lee Myung-bak administration's emphasis on denuclearization brings U.S. and South Korean policies closer in line with each other. At the same time, it is possible that South Korea's aversion to coercive or military options that might lead to instability on the peninsula could come into conflict with American measures to pursue counterproliferation or prevent transfers that might enable nuclear terrorism.

The Lee administration's prudent and careful response to the suspicious sinking of a South Korean corvette in disputed waters in the West Sea on March 26, 2010—starting with the establishment of an international investigation team and its determination to work closely with the United States in responding to the incident—has further bolstered confidence in Washington regarding President Lee's leadership and commitment to the alliance. This incident will require continued close coordination between the United States and South Korea, including joint consultations on available response options now that North Korea is indisputably tied to the incident. As a practical matter, the incident will effectively suspend any diplomatic engagement with

North Korea until the South Korean government is prepared to resume those efforts.

CONTINGENCY PLANNING

North Korea's refusal to return to the path of denuclearization heightens the prospect of diplomatic confrontation and rising regional tensions. Moreover, North Korea's economic situation remains dire because the regime is unable to provide for the needs of its people. In addition, Kim Jong-il's efforts to establish a hereditary succession by designating his third son as his successor may or may not succeed. Given the uncertainties and associated risks related to North Korea's future, it is necessary and sensible for its neighbors to consider the possibility of volatility in North Korea and plan for its possible effects.

Planning for contingencies in North Korea is not the same as predicting instability or pursuing a policy that induces instability; however, it is prudent to consider how to respond to instability as part of the full range of possible outcomes in dealing with North Korea.[29] Contingency planning also provides an opportunity to identify potential areas of misunderstanding or disagreement between the United States, South Korea, and others, improve coordination mechanisms, and identify needed resources. Moreover, participating in dialogue about future scenarios reassures China, Japan, and South Korea that their concerns about instability are being taken seriously. Believing that the negative repercussions of increased pressure on North Korea will be satisfactorily managed may allow them to consider stronger, tougher measures against North Korea.

It is difficult to know with certainty what will happen in North Korea as a result of a leadership succession; there is a strong possibility, however, that a contested or failed succession would lead to a breakdown of political control and the development of humanitarian or other challenges. These would pose political, security, or humanitarian spillover effects to North Korea's neighbors, principally South Korea and China.

Contingency planning is made more challenging by the fact that no neighbor of North Korea wants to be seen as pursuing such a plan at the expense of diplomacy. Planning for Kim's departure feeds North Korean paranoia about the intentions of its neighbors. The Task Force believes that the United States and South Korea should deepen quiet discussions to forge a "whole-of-alliance" approach—which should then be expanded to include Japan, and then China and Russia—to enhance preparedness to respond to potential political instability in the North.[30] As discussed in the China section, the Task Force also calls for a U.S. strategic dialogue with China to discuss the future of the peninsula.

These discussions would develop a shared understanding of the various challenges, the preferred responses and objectives of the parties, the available resources that might be brought to bear to contain instability and restore security, and how to avoid the use of nuclear weapons and ensure the security of North Korea's nuclear weapons and nuclear materials in the event of lost central government control.

The establishment of discussions on these issues would provide an important opportunity to clear misunderstanding, build trust, and develop plans that would reduce the possibility of uncoordinated or conflicting responses to instability in North Korea.

A Comprehensive Agenda

This Task Force's primary focus has been on how the United States and its allies should respond to North Korea's nuclear development; however, several other issues on the bilateral agenda have received relatively little international attention but must also be addressed. North Korea's missile program is a significant concern because advancements in this area will allow North Korea to deliver a nuclear weapon. In addition, the abysmal human rights situation in North Korea looms large. Finally, a persistent challenge for the United States has been how to improve the effectiveness of humanitarian aid to the North Korean people.

NORTH KOREA'S MISSILE DEVELOPMENT EFFORTS

As North Korea's nuclear tests have drawn attention from the United States and the international community, its missile development has proceeded in parallel. North Korea's missile development has drawn censure, but the George W. Bush administration chose not to address missiles as part of the six-party agenda. The Task Force emphasizes that stopping North Korea's missile development should be a high-priority issue for the Obama administration and the international community. The threat of North Korea's missile program cannot be overstated. The development of an adequate delivery capacity would enable North Korea to expand the scope of its arsenal and threaten or actually deliver a nuclear strike to its neighbors.

North Korea's intercontinental missile capability emerged as a significant concern in August 1998, when North Korea launched its first Taepodong missile in an effort it claimed was the launch of a satellite. In 2006, the North Koreans tested a multistage missile, but the test failed less than a minute after the launch. North Korea has also conducted periodic tests of short- and medium-range missiles since 2006, especially in 2009. There has been occasional discussion of the need to add missiles to the six-party agenda, but the issue has not been formally taken up, in part because the nuclear issue has been deemed more urgent.

North Korea's earlier announcement of a multistage rocket launch carrying an artificial satellite payload in April 2009 was designed to evade international censure. The reasons for this test appear to have been driven by internal political considerations related to North Korea's efforts to put into place a leadership succession process from Kim Jong-il to his third son, Kim Jong-eun. North Korea launched a similar missile test in the week before Kim Jong-il's formal assumption of power in September 1998, presumably as a show of strength. The April 2009 test, only hours before Obama's speech in Prague announcing his commitment to promoting global nuclear weapons reductions, drew immediate condemnation from the Obama administration and the international community.

Given the need to constrain North Korean missile development and the fact that efforts to address the missile issue have not previously been a part of the six-party agenda, the Task Force recommends that the United States pursue bilateral negotiations with North Korea confined to the missile issue and separate from denuclearization talks, which should occur in the six-party framework. The first task of this negotiating effort would be to convince the DPRK to recommit to a moratorium on missile tests as negotiations over its nuclear and missile programs continue. North Korea's expanded missile delivery capacity must be factored in to South Korean defense efforts, including strengthening missile defense and developing additional response capabilities necessary to offset that capability.

At the same time, the United States should continue to strengthen missile defense coordination with Japan and South Korea to install proper defenses against any expansion in North Korean capabilities. With the consent of Japan and South Korea, the United States might consider declaring a willingness to pursue preemptive actions against future North Korean missile launches to reinforce existing UN Security Council resolutions against North Korean long-range missile tests.[31]

Of concern to the United States is the potential for North Korea to proliferate its existing weapons materials and technologies to other state or nonstate actors, particularly Iran. North Korea and Iran are known to have shared technology and information with each other as part of their respective missile development programs.[32] And there are strong suspicions that cooperation between them extends to the nuclear field, including possibly both uranium- and plutonium-based nuclear development efforts.[33]

Cooperation in the missile field is long-standing and well known, with North Korean and Iranian scientists reportedly even present to observe their respective missile tests. In addition, there are indications that North Korea's technical assistance to Syria to build a small-scale nuclear plant for plutonium production may have been leaked to Iran. Some estimates of the value of North Korea-Iran annual trade in these illicit areas run as high as $2 billion in recent years.[34]

The possibility of further cooperation is of great concern to the United States and the international community. It directly challenges international norms embodied by the NPT, defies UNSC Resolutions 1718 and 1874, and challenges the capacity of member states to implement UNSC Resolution 1540, which requires cooperation to prevent the international transfer of fissile materials.[35] UNSC Resolution 1874 seeks to prevent additional DPRK imports of sensitive technologies or components that might be used to improve North Korea's missile development capabilities.[36] The Task Force calls on all parties to implement these measures strictly in order to constrain further progress in North Korea's development of a missile delivery capability or risk facing the consequences that would result from an even more dangerous North Korea with the capability to deliver a nuclear device to any part of South Korea or Japan.

HUMAN RIGHTS

The Task Force continues to be deeply concerned about deplorable conditions in North Korea and strongly decries human rights abuses under the current regime. As the leadership has enriched itself and operated a vast prison camp system to control the population and punish its political enemies, the North Korean people have suffered extreme poverty and devastating famines that have led to food shortages and lack of essential services. The totalitarian regime asserts almost complete control over its populace and does not allow basic political freedoms. Free speech is severely curtailed and any perceived opposition to or criticism of the leadership is brutally suppressed.[37]

North Korea has routinely been cited as having the world's worst human rights practices by the Heritage Foundation's Freedom Index and other global surveys.[38] The United States cannot seek to improve relations with North Korea without taking significant steps to bring its human rights conditions up to international standards. Not addressing North Korea's most serious human rights failings will also make it impossible for the U.S. Congress to cooperate with the U.S. administration to provide financial support for any effort to improve U.S.-DPRK bilateral relations.

The North denounces criticism of its human rights record as anti–North Korean propaganda designed to undermine its regime and attack its legitimacy. Yet it appears susceptible to international criticisms of its human rights policies, as illustrated by the North Korean media's defensive responses and the regime's (failing) efforts to keep the worst human rights practices hidden from international scrutiny. Indeed, the Kim regime's desperate desire for international recognition and approbation may offer an opening for increased efforts to improve the lot of its people.

There has been almost no success in establishing official channels for dialogue on human rights with the DPRK. However, international activism designed to draw public attention to, and thereby increase, international pressure to deal with North Korean human rights abuses has grown, fueled by an increasing flow of North Korean refugees to South Korea during the past decade. The number of North Korean defectors to the South passed 16,000 in 2009, according to the ROK Ministry of Unification, with annual flows reaching more than 3,000.[39]

American human rights activists have played a major role in drawing international attention to the cause of North Korean human rights since the late 1990s by bringing North Korean refugees to Capitol Hill to spotlight their stories, developing a global network of activists dedicated to the issue, and publishing research on important aspects of North Korean human rights suppression, including the appalling situation in North Korean concentration camps. These efforts have catalyzed attention to the North Korean human rights issue in the U.S. Congress and led to the passage of the North Korean Human Rights

Act in 2004 and a revised act in 2008. This legislation has encouraged the U.S. government to accept more North Korean refugees for resettlement in the United States, promoted the appointment of a North Korea human rights envoy, and authorized some funding in support of organizations that have promoted human rights advocacy or been involved in providing assistance to North Korean refugees in their efforts to come to the United States.

The Task Force applauds U.S. congressional efforts to call attention to these concerns. It is important that North Korea's human rights situation be addressed as a critical issue in any U.S.-DPRK bilateral talks and that the U.S. administration's human rights envoy participate as a full member of the negotiating team in future negotiations with North Korea. Human rights efforts should not be linked to nuclear negotiations but should be a part of any U.S.-DPRK bilateral negotiation on the improvement of diplomatic relations. The U.S. human rights envoy should actively support international efforts to pressure North Korea for failing to live up to international standards, and the United States should increase its investment in Korean language radio programming and other efforts to disseminate information to the North Korean people.

HUMANITARIAN AID

North Korea's systemic failure to provide enough food to meet the needs of its people has resulted in a chronic need for imports from its neighbors and the international community. A famine prompted by natural disasters and economic mismanagement killed hundreds of thousands of North Koreans in the 1990s. North Korea's food situation has worsened following the country's botched 2009 currency revaluation and accompanying confiscatory measures, leading to further impoverishment and fueled inflation.

In recent months, South Korea has restricted donations of fertilizer and rice that had been supplied on a humanitarian basis under the engagement policies of previous governments. In addition, the North Korean leadership abruptly halted U.S.-funded international food relief through the UN World Food Program and through various American nongovernmental organizations (NGOs). Moreover, the worldwide price of grains on the international market has risen, influencing the price and availability of grain in North Korea's farmers' markets.

The people of North Korea cannot be left to suffer the consequences of its leadership's failures without a response from the international community. The United States signaled recently that it would consider resuming food aid to North Korea if Pyongyang moves to lift the year-old refusal of its humanitarian assistance.

Food aid—mainly from China, the United States, and South Korea—has been essential in addressing North Korea's chronic food deficits for more than a decade. The United States has provided North Korea with more than $1.2 billion in aid since 1995, about 60 percent of which has paid for food aid and 40 percent for energy aid.[40] The Task Force notes that humanitarian aid to North Korea has had several benefits, including helping to meet the urgent needs of the North Korean people, underscoring American support for the people of North Korea while upholding American ideals, limiting refugee flows, and socializing North Korean authorities to international standards for provision of assistance.

Future humanitarian aid provision should be structured so that it does not strengthen the North Korean leadership and does not damage the existing important role of farmers' markets in North Korean daily life. Reports have indicated a high level of North Korean dependency on external aid and evidence of aid diversion to the military or of resale in the market. But the United States can provide aid in ways that maximize humanitarian benefits while limiting manipulation by the regime, such as providing lower-quality grains not preferred by the North Korean elite and targeting aid geographically, though it is difficult for the United States to independently determine where the greatest needs exist.[41]

In considering the resumption of food aid to the North, the Obama administration must also consider whether to condition assistance on access and monitoring and whether to pressure China to base food aid on similar conditions.[42] The Task Force supports past U.S. government efforts to condition humanitarian assistance on the DPRK's acceptance of internationally accepted standards for monitoring and delivery to ensure that aid is delivered to the intended recipients. It recommends that all states coordinate and implement conditions for monitoring of humanitarian aid consistent with international standards. North Korean authorities have thus far resisted efforts to conduct independent nutrition surveys to evaluate the overall health and needs of the population, and have instead determined the distribution end points for aid and imposed restrictions on monitoring.

Another challenge of aid is that though the market is the most effective means of distributing food, assistance may have market-distorting effects. Efforts should be made to promote the financing of small-scale development projects and micro-lending in local communities, pending the negotiation of international accountability and monitoring standards and joint technical implementation of such programs by NGOs.

U.S.-South Korea Relations

Strong alliance coordination with South Korea has ensured peninsular stability for more than five decades, initially in response to North Korea's conventional threat and now in promoting a coordinated response to North Korea's efforts to develop nuclear weapons. While successfully deterring North Korea, the alliance also provided the political stability necessary for South Korea's economic and political transformation into a leading market economy with a vibrant democratic political system. South Korea's democratic transformation has allowed a more robust and enduring partnership with the United States that also applies to a growing list of regional and global security, economic, and political issues beyond North Korea.

Presidents Obama and Lee recognized the potential for such cooperation through the adoption of a Joint Vision Statement at their White House meeting in June 2009.[43] Citing shared values between the two countries, the statement outlines an agenda for broadened global cooperation on peacekeeping, postconflict stabilization, and development assistance, as well as for addressing a wide range of common challenges to human security, including "terrorism, proliferation of weapons of mass destruction, piracy, organized crime and narcotics, climate change, poverty, infringement on human rights, energy security, and epidemic disease."[44]

The Joint Vision Statement also underscores U.S. commitments to defend South Korea from North Korea's nuclear challenge by providing extended deterrence to protect South Korea—that is, a pledge to use its nuclear arsenal in response to any nuclear attack on South Korea—and to transition the role of U.S. forces in South Korea from a leading to a supporting role. It also pledges to strengthen bilateral economic, trade, and investment ties through ratification of the Korea-U.S. Free Trade Agreement (KORUS FTA).

The Task Force believes that the Joint Vision Statement constitutes a valuable foundation for U.S.-ROK cooperation and should be implemented fully. The Korean decision in late 2009 to provide a Provincial Reconstruction Team (PRT) to Afghanistan is a welcome contribution to the global security issue at the top of the Obama administration's agenda, and South Korea's role as host and chair of the Group of Twenty (G20) summit in 2010 and the 2012 nuclear security summit is a basis on which the United States and South Korea can build cooperation to manage recovery from the global financial crisis.

The role of the alliance as a platform for constructive South Korean regional diplomacy is likely to become more important in the context of rising Chinese influence. When paired with the U.S.-Japan alliance, which is based on a complementary set of values and interests, the U.S.-led alliance system in Northeast Asia is a cornerstone for regional stability and provides a framework for promoting East Asian security cooperation.

This report highlights two pending issues in the Joint Vision Statement that need attention: the implementation of revised operational control (OPCON) arrangements set to take place by April 17, 2012, and the ratification of the KORUS FTA facing both legislatures.

REVISED ARRANGEMENTS
FOR OPERATIONAL CONTROL

U.S. forces have been stationed in South Korea since the end of the Korean War in 1953. The South Korea-U.S. Combined Forces Command (CFC) was established in 1978 to manage combined forces. The United States Forces Korea (USFK) includes ground, air, and naval divisions of the U.S. armed forces. The presence of U.S. troops on the peninsula has served both as a reassurance to the people of South Korea and as a point of contention among competing political parties in South Korea.

A decision to revise OPCON arrangements, including dismantling the CFC structure and replacing it with separate South Korean and U.S. commands in Korea, was initiated by the Roh Moo-hyun administration. Roh's progressive administration believed that the existing CFC arrangement both impinged on South Korea's sovereignty and underscored the inherent inequality of the U.S.-ROK alliance relationship. Many Korean conservatives, including some retired generals' and veterans' associations, opposed the decision on the grounds that the move would weaken South Korea's deterrent against the North; they gathered almost ten million signatures in a campaign protesting the new arrangements.

The George W. Bush administration and Defense Secretary Donald Rumsfeld accepted the Roh administration's initiative and put it on a fast track, with both sides agreeing at a 2007 Security Consultative Meeting to put revised OPCON arrangements into effect between March of 2010 and April 17, 2012.[45] USFK and the South Korean Ministry of National Defense have implemented preparations for the revision, using annual joint exercises to test new arrangements and assess the ability of both sides to communicate with each other effectively. The Task Force does not contest the decision to implement new arrangements but believes that the transfer should not be rushed.

A number of adjustments have been made to ensure continuity of capabilities and a smooth transition to the new arrangements. These include the decision to maintain a single, coordinated operational plan for responding to North Korean aggression, to continue using the U.S. command, control, communications, computers, and intelligence (C^4I) platform for the foreseeable future, and to continue supporting the ROK in the provision of air and intelligence capabilities in the event of a conflict.

While applauding the efforts of the two militaries to prepare for OPCON transfer, the Task Force believes that the chief criterion for its implementation should be condition rather than deadline based. The deadline comes during a presidential election year in South Korea, running the risk that the issue could be politicized during the campaign. Additionally, the Task Force notes that the April 17 deadline falls only two days after the hundredth anniversary of Kim Il-sung's birth, creating an opportunity for the DPRK to exploit the transfer for domestic propaganda purposes by declaring that the United States is retreating in the face of North Korea's increasing strength.

RATIFICATION OF KORUS FTA

KORUS FTA is the United States' first free trade agreement with a major Asian economy and its largest trade deal since the North American Free Trade Agreement (NAFTA). The agreement would lift some 85 percent of each nation's tariffs on industrial goods. The KORUS

FTA was negotiated under the George W. Bush and Roh Moo-Hyun administrations, but neither administration had submitted the agreement for legislative ratification by the end of their respective terms. As of now, it has not been approved by either the U.S. Congress or the National Assembly of South Korea.

The Task Force strongly supports the agreement. The benefits to both sides would be substantial—it would be good for U.S. companies and would strengthen the U.S.-Korea relationship—and the repercussions of failing to ratify it would be significant. The Task Force concedes that it will be a tough sell to the U.S. Congress amid the current partisan political climate, especially as the midterm elections approach. The Democratic Party has also traditionally been opposed to free trade agreements. Nonetheless, the Task Force considers the stakes and advantages to be sufficiently high and urges the Obama administration to push for the deal's ratification in 2011.

Initial obstacles to congressional consideration of the KORUS FTA in 2008 were Korean restrictions on U.S. beef imports and prohibitive tariffs and taxes on the sales of U.S. vehicles.[46] Although the KORUS FTA did not directly cover beef exports, senators from beef-exporting states made clear that KORUS would not be considered until South Korea resumed imports of American beef, which had been excluded from the market since December 2003 over concerns and protests about an isolated case of mad cow disease.[47] The South Korean government eventually worked out a deal with the United States under which the beef market was partially and incrementally opened, and in the summer of 2008 public protests began to die down.

After the 2008 U.S. elections, the global financial crisis and its impact on the American economy dealt another setback to congressional support for free trade in 2009. The Obama administration has faced multiple challenges and priorities during its first year in office that have been more important than the KORUS FTA, including managing a response to the global financial crisis and pursuing domestic healthcare reform. President Obama clearly indicated to President Lee in June 2009 that healthcare took priority over the FTA. Though the South Korean government has shown considerable patience and understanding regarding U.S. domestic priorities, it cannot be expected to wait indefinitely, and indeed its leaders have voiced increasing frustration in recent months.[48]

The KORUS FTA faces strong opposition from some of the Obama administration's core constituencies, including labor. Congressional opposition to the KORUS FTA has primarily come from representatives with close ties to the auto sector, which worries about Korean competition. Additional negotiations between the United States and South Korea will be necessary to address concerns regarding several auto sector provisions in the agreement, but they have not yet taken place, in part because the Obama administration has been slow to establish a clear policy on trade.[49] At this stage, there is no reliable prediction regarding the timing of intergovernmental negotiations or when the administration might formally submit the agreement to Congress for ratification.

The Task Force believes that the KORUS FTA would enhance the competitiveness of American companies in South Korea and in Asia. Failure to ratify it would give other countries an advantage over the United States in the growing South Korean market. Congress would do well to note that South Korea and the European Union (EU) recently forged an FTA that uses the same template as the one used for negotiation of the KORUS FTA.[50] If the Korea-EU agreement goes into force first, EU companies will have an advantage over U.S. competitors in a range of sectors because they will enjoy lower Korean tariffs than their American counterparts.[51]

China uses FTAs to strengthen its political relations in Asia, but most of its agreements do not include trade liberalization measures. By holding up the KORUS FTA, Congress is placing the United States at a disadvantage by losing the opportunity to drive Asian trade liberalization and allowing China to set the pace on regional trade arrangements. China is currently pressing South Korea to join a three-way Northeast Asian trade arrangement that would form the basis of an Asian bloc that may ultimately prove discriminatory to U.S. market access.

The KORUS FTA also helps bind the United States and South Korea more closely together strategically, economically, and politically.[52] The economic significance of the KORUS FTA is substantial, but the opportunity to bring South Korea closer to the United States as a partner—especially given that China is currently South Korea's primary trade and investment partner—is significant. Failure to approve the agreement would send a negative message: that despite South Korea's role and significance as one of the top twenty economies in the world, there are limits to U.S. economic and, by extension, strategic cooperation with South Korea. Following U.S. midterm elections and in the context of steady U.S. economic improvement, ratification of the KORUS FTA should be a top Obama administration priority for 2011.

Recommendations

North Korea's bid to gain international recognition as a nuclear weapons state has negative ramifications for global, regional, and peninsular stability. The United States must pursue a comprehensive North Korean strategy to prevent onward proliferation, block vertical proliferation, and press for denuclearization. Despite the Obama administration's rhetorical support for these objectives, its commitment seems to be intermittent.

The Task Force supports the Obama administration's efforts to build regional cohesion, premised on strong U.S.-ROK and U.S.-Japan alliance-based policy coordination, as the basis for a collective approach to denuclearization of the Korean peninsula through the Six Party Talks.

The Task Force urges continued efforts to secure China's cooperation, including the development of a strategic understanding between the United States and China that is based on prior consultations with allies in South Korea and Japan. Based on shared interests in regional stability and a nonnuclear Korean peninsula, the United States should attempt to allay China's suspicions of its strategic intentions in order to expand the basis for cooperation to denuclearize the Korean peninsula.

To best address North Korea's continuing nuclear challenge, the United States needs to provide political leadership in cooperation with regional counterparts to roll back North Korea's nuclear development, coordinate actions designed to contain the spillover effects of possible North Korean instability while insisting that North Korea give up its destabilizing course of action, and affirm that one prerequisite to a normal U.S.-DPRK relationship is a denuclearized North Korea.

The Task Force is concerned about the potential repercussions of the sinking of the South Korean warship in March 2010. The findings of the international investigation, which blamed North Korea for firing a torpedo that sank Seoul's warship and killed forty-six sailors, were released as this report went to press. The Task Force applauds South Korea's careful investigation and close coordination with the United

States and supports efforts to prevent escalation. The Task Force is sympathetic to Seoul's imposition of sanctions against the North and endorses the move to take the incident to the UNSC. The Task Force acknowledges that a resumption of negotiations is unlikely in the near future, as long as tensions between the two Koreas remain high.

U.S. PRIORITIES

The Task Force believes that the Obama administration should deal with North Korea's policy challenges in the following order:

- *Prevent horizontal proliferation.* North Korea's nuclear weapons program poses a serious horizontal proliferation threat, as evidenced by its documented exports to Libya and to Syria and by the potential of nuclear exports to or cooperation with Iran. The United States must also be concerned that a failing regime or new leadership in North Korea might sell fissile material to the highest bidder, and about a situation in which control of its stockpile of fissile material could be jeopardized. North Korean horizontal proliferation would potentially result in a direct threat to U.S. national security and regional stability.

- *Stop vertical proliferation.* North Korea's continued vertical proliferation efforts, including the conduct of additional long-range missile or nuclear tests, will eventually allow it to acquire the ability to deliver a nuclear weapon on its missiles and hold Japan and some U.S. assets at risk. It could also potentially lead to a response expansion of nuclear weapons states in northeast Asia.

- *Denuclearize.* North Korea's bid for nuclear weapons status poses a challenge to the global nuclear nonproliferation regime and sets a worrisome precedent for other states that might consider challenging the regime.

- *Plan for contingencies.* Potential North Korean instability, including the possibility of refugee flows, loss of regime control over nuclear weapons or fissile material, and prolonged internal chaos, would have a negative influence on regional stability and affect the dynamics of interstate relations in Northeast Asia.

- *Promote engagement.* North Korea's isolation sustains the political control of the current leadership, whereas exposure to the outside world could eventually lead to regime transformation. Expanded educational exchanges and broadened access to information about the outside world will increase the likelihood that the North Korean people will see beyond the lies iterated by their leaders and insist on North Korea's integration with the rest of the world.

– *Improve the situation for the North Korean people.* North Korea's shameful human rights situation and failure to meet the needs of its people is a human tragedy that should be addressed by U.S. humanitarian assistance and other measures to improve human rights conditions inside North Korea.

The Task Force finds that the efforts taken thus far by the United States and its partners are insufficient to fully prevent North Korea's onward or vertical proliferation or to roll back its nuclear program. The United States must seek to resolve rather than simply manage the challenge posed by a nuclear North Korea. Resolving these issues would also allow the implementation of an effective U.S. humanitarian and human rights policy toward North Korea.

CONTAIN HORIZONTAL PROLIFERATION

The United States and its allies should heighten vigilance against the possibility of a transfer of nuclear weapons technologies or fissile material from North Korea and strengthen the capacity to carry out effective counterproliferation measures. This effort requires greater coordination and more intrusive measures toward North Korea by the international community as part of the implementation of UNSC Resolution 1874. In addition, activities undertaken under the Proliferation Security Initiative (PSI), a voluntary effort by states to enhance coordination and expand their capacity to prevent proliferation, are designed to prevent transfer of nuclear-related materials.

The United States should inform North Korea that any instance of horizontal proliferation—or any incident of nuclear terrorism involving the unexplained transfer of nuclear materials to nonstate actors—is a direct threat to the United States and would potentially invite direct retaliation, following the model of the September 2007 Israeli strike on a North Korean–model nuclear reactor under construction in Syria.

- The United States should lead efforts with its allies under UNSC Resolution 1874 to strengthen export controls and monitor trade with North Korea to prevent the import of sensitive dual-use technologies to limit, if not cap, North Korea's nuclear weapons and missile development efforts.

- Full implementation of Resolution 1874 would also limit North Korean exports of nuclear or missile-related technologies through interdiction activities, serve notice to potential customers that transfers from North Korea are under strict scrutiny, and pressure North Korea to return to the path of denuclearization.

- The decision to appoint Ambassador Philip Goldberg as coordinator for the implementation of UNSC Resolution 1874 provided initial focus and evidence of the Obama administration's commitment to implement the UN resolution in the months following its adoption by the Security Council. However, with Goldberg's subsequent appointment as the State Department's assistant secretary for intelligence and research, the spotlight within the administration appears to have shifted away from implementation. The Task Force recommends that the Obama administration continue active efforts to implement UNSC Resolution 1874, either by continuing Goldberg's active attention to this issue or appointing another high-level official with the responsibility for ongoing efforts to promote sanctions implementation.

CONTAIN VERTICAL PROLIFERATION

North Korea's unconstrained efforts to develop a missile delivery capability for its nuclear arsenal would dramatically expand its ability to threaten its neighbors and further complicate prospects for reversing its nuclear program.

- The Task Force recommends that the Obama administration test North Korean willingness to open bilateral negotiations on a permanent missile testing moratorium by authorizing high-level bilateral negotiations with North Korea confined to the specific task of negotiating a missile moratorium. The opening of bilateral missile negotiations would provide an opportunity for direct U.S.-DPRK interaction—to avoid dependence on China as an intermediary—without compromising the Six Party Talks as the appropriate venue for denuclearization talks.

- Bilateral missile negotiations should seek a moratorium on North Korean missile development activities in return for reversible U.S. assurances and steps designed to show that U.S. policy toward North Korea is not hostile, such as the establishment of a liaison office in North Korea.

- Specific forms of humanitarian and energy assistance along the lines of generators provided for use in North Korean hospitals might be provided to North Korea as inducements, as long as they are delivered in conformity with international standards for the provision of humanitarian aid.

- The United States should lead efforts to broaden the scope and strength of UNSC resolutions in the event that North Korea's continued missile development results in violations of the resolutions already on the books.

- North Korea's missile development should be dealt with through stepped-up export controls of critical components that might facilitate the technical capacity of North Korea to develop medium- and long-range missiles.

- The United States and Japan should consult on measures to address North Korea's medium- and long-range missiles, including the existing deployments of an estimated three hundred Rodong missiles capable of reaching Japan. These midrange missiles have not been included in past efforts to freeze North Korean development of intercontinental ballistic missile technology but have a direct bearing on Japan's security.

- The United States and Japan should continue to develop missile defense capabilities as one measure that should protect Japan from the possibility of a missile strike from North Korea. The United States should also extend its cooperation on missile defense to South Korea in response to North Korea's deployment of short- and midrange missiles.

PRESS FOR DENUCLEARIZATION

The Task Force finds that a nuclear-capable North Korea under its current leadership threatens the credibility of the global nonproliferation regime and undermines Northeast Asia's stability. An approach that attempts to contain the risks of North Korean proliferation while managing to freeze nuclear and missile capabilities at their current levels is necessary, but the Task Force finds that these steps are not enough to achieve full denuclearization of the Korean peninsula. The Task Force finds that the debate over nonproliferation versus denuclearization is a false choice; the United States and its partners can and must do both by containing proliferation while also pressing for denuclearization.

The Task Force recommends a denuclearization strategy that includes elements of both coercion and diplomacy, requiring close consultations by the United States with allies and partners in its implementation. The Task Force affirms that the United States must take the lead in building a consensus to address the North Korean issue as a high priority, particularly given the implications for dealing with nuclear challenges in Iran.

- Regional cohesion (solving problems through multilateral talks) will be a prerequisite for movement on denuclearization. The United States should embed denuclearization objectives within a larger framework designed to lay the foundation for regional stability. In this regard, the United States should continue to make it clear to North Korea that there is no prospect of diplomatic normalization without denuclearization.

- The Obama administration should develop plans to achieve North Korea's denuclearization within the next five years and launch commensurate efforts to achieve that objective. Such an approach would strengthen the credibility of the administration's commitment to denuclearization of the Korean peninsula. Any acceptance of a longer time frame would imply that the United States and North Korea's neighbors are willing to live with a nuclear weapons–capable North Korea.

- The U.S. administration should, while working toward denuclearization, prioritize "three *nos*" as primary objectives in dealing with

North Korea: no export of nuclear technologies, no more bombs, and no "better" bombs. The administration should pursue counterprolif-eration aggressively through implementation of UN resolutions. At the same time, it should take steps to prevent any further enhance-ments of North Korea's nuclear program by negotiating a bilateral missile moratorium and strengthening counterproliferation efforts to constrain North Korea's capacity to build more bombs or improve its existing arsenal.

– The United States should continue to pursue diplomatic engagement with North Korea backed by coordinated pressure among North Korea's neighbors to implement the objectives of denuclearization, reduce regional tension, improve U.S.-DPRK relations (including the replacement of the Korean armistice with permanent peace arrange-ments on the Korean peninsula), provide economic and energy assis-tance, and integrate North Korea into Northeast Asia.

– The United States should make it clear to North Korea that as the only nuclear weapons state outside the NPT framework, it will be consid-ered suspect number one whenever nuclear material is found in the hands of nonstate actors or in any incident involving nuclear terror-ism. The United States should declare in advance of such an incident that, as long as North Korea is not pursuing denuclearization, it would consider a retaliatory strike against North Korea—as one of the most likely sources of nuclear materials that might enable such terrorism—or a shift to active advocacy of DPRK regime change.

PLAN FOR CONTINGENCIES

The Task Force finds that North Korea's actions have heightened the need for contingency planning. Discussions with partners should take place with the understanding that though none of the parties seeks instability in North Korea, the political, security, and broader ramifica-tions of North Korea's destabilizing role in the region compel coordi-nated preparations to limit the external impact of potential instability. The Task Force believes that a discussion among North Korea's neigh-bors would also have positive effects in building regional cooperation.

To better plan for and coordinate responses to potential scenarios on the Korean peninsula, the Task Force recommends the following steps.

- The United States should deepen discussions with South Korea to identify the obligations of each party related to the pursuit of a democratic, market-oriented unification of the Korean peninsula. Both sides should agree on criteria that would require U.S.-ROK intervention in North Korea in the event of a system collapse. The United States and South Korea should clarify to China the June 2009 U.S.-ROK Joint Vision Statement and how it is to be implemented. The United States and South Korea should pursue political coordination regarding their possible responses to regime, system, or state failure in North Korea and design a "whole-of-alliance" response that is coordinated among political and military officials on each side.

- Given its role as a neighboring state whose interests will be affected by North Korean instability, Japan should be brought into U.S.-ROK discussions at an early stage as an ally of the United States and as the provider of logistical support for any military response to volatile scenarios on the Korean peninsula.

- Based on a clear understanding of U.S.-ROK objectives related to the future of the Korean peninsula, the United States should initiate a high-level strategic dialogue with China on the future of North Korea and how to prevent it from provoking instability that might spread to the greater region. Following this conversation, the two leaders should authorize a three-way dialogue between the U.S., Chinese, and South Korean governments on the situation in North Korea and how the three might respond to the regional and spillover effects of North Korean instability.

PROMOTE ENGAGEMENT

The nuclear stalemate has constrained the U.S. government's ability to promote actions that facilitate North Korea's economic opening and integration into the international community. U.S. policies, however, should not restrict nongovernmental activities designed to promote enhanced North Korean understanding of the outside world or that can stimulate change inside North Korea. The Task Force recommends that the Obama administration pursue forms of engagement with North Korea that are likely to bring about change in the country, regardless of the policies of the North Korean leadership.

- North Koreans should be encouraged to participate in nongovernmental exchange programs in the United States in nontechnical areas
  on an unconditional basis without regard to the immediate political
  environment and subject to existing review and approval by the U.S.
  Department of Homeland Security.

- The Obama administration should adopt a visa policy that provides maximum space for nongovernmental forms of engagement
  designed to bring North Koreans to the United States for exchanges
  in a wide range of fields. Political approvals for cultural, sports, and
  educational exchanges should be approved on a routine basis.

- The administration should continue funding for Korean-language
  radio broadcasts that promote the dissemination of information
  inside North Korea and for programs designed to provide safe passage for North Korean refugees out of China.

- The administration should promote the establishment of a scholarship fund for North Koreans to pursue advanced academic training
  at U.S. academic institutions. Existing U.S. government–funded
  scholarship programs, such as the Department of Agriculture–
  sponsored Borlaug Fellows program and the Fulbright program,
  should be expanded to include North Korean participation in a wide
  range of areas—as long as the subjects of study are unrelated to the
  nuclear science and advanced engineering fields or any other field
  that might have application to North Korea's military, nuclear, or
  missile development programs.[53]

- The Obama administration should change long-standing U.S. policies blocking North Korea's participation in activities of international
  financial institutions. Technical requirements for formal membership in such organizations will require North Korea to provide
  effective reporting to the international financial system. The United
  States, Japan, and South Korea should support activities designed to
  prepare North Korea for membership in IFIs in the context of North
  Korea's continued commitment to and tangible progress toward
  denuclearization.

IMPROVE HUMAN RIGHTS

The Task Force is concerned about the appalling conditions in North
Korea and condemns human rights abuses under the current regime.

North Korean performance on human rights–related issues is a direct concern of the United States and must be addressed as an important issue in the bilateral relationship. The Task Force supports U.S. congressional efforts to call attention to these concerns through the passage of the 2004 North Korean Human Rights Act.

- The Task Force supports international efforts to pursue broadly based and persistent international pressure on the North Korean government to meet its obligations to its people according to international standards. The Task Force applauds the broad array of private efforts to mobilize international pressure on North Korea through a variety of forums that publicly call on North Korea to meet international human rights standards.

- The U.S. government should expand funding for efforts to inform the North Korean people about conditions outside North Korea through the Korean-language services of the Voice of America and Radio Free Asia.

- The U.S. government should extend financial support for the education of North Korean refugees in anticipation that they may play a pivotal role under a transformed regime that embraces openness and reform.

- China should live up to its obligations under international treaties to not repatriate North Korean refugees without providing an opportunity for international examination and review of their status by the UN High Commission for Refugees.

- The U.S. Congress should adopt Sullivan Principles—analogous to those that imposed human rights standards on companies investing in South Africa under apartheid—designed to hold private sector investors accountable for investments they might make in North Korea.

- North Korea's human rights situation should be addressed as an important issue in any U.S.-DPRK bilateral talks. Such efforts should not be linked to nuclear negotiations but should be a part of any bilateral negotiation on improvement of diplomatic relations. To that end, the administration's current human rights envoy, Robert R. King, should participate as a full member of the North Korean negotiating team in future negotiations.

- North Korea's chronic food crisis is a symptom of a failed ideology that promotes self-sufficiency despite the country's inability to produce enough food to meet the needs of its people. The greater population of North Korea cannot be left to suffer the consequences of its leadership's failures without a response from the international community. The Task Force recommends that, if North Korea requests it, the United States and South Korea resume humanitarian aid, structuring it so as not to strengthen the North Korean leadership or damage the existing role of farmers' markets in North Korean daily life.

- The U.S. government should, when providing humanitarian assistance to North Korea, allow aid providers to secure food through Chinese markets close to North Korea. The U.S. government should continue to provide lower-quality grains not favored by the elite, to prevent siphoning, and distribute aid on a priority basis to peripheral areas far from Pyongyang that are not prioritized by the North Korean government.

- Efforts should be made to promote the financing of small-scale development projects and micro-lending in local communities, pending the negotiation of international accountability and monitoring standards and joint technical implementation of such programs by nongovernmental organizations.

U.S.-CHINA COOPERATION

Chinese cooperation is essential to the success of denuclearization on the Korean peninsula and to ensuring regional stability. Sino-U.S. cooperation to prevent proliferation of weapons of mass destruction (WMD) is in the mutual interests of both countries and will be a critical proving ground for the relationship. Failure to make progress toward denuclearization of the Korean peninsula would be a significant setback for efforts to promote a cooperative approach to regional security in Northeast Asia. The level of China's cooperation and involvement is the main factor that will determine whether it is possible to achieve a strategy that goes beyond containment and management of North Korea's nuclear and missile aspirations to rollback.

The United States should pursue the following measures designed to enhance prospects for China's cooperation in dealing with North Korea.

- Determine that it is a top priority in U.S.-China relations to make progress in bringing North Korea back to the path of denuclearization.

- Engage China, on the basis of prior consultations with allies South Korea and Japan, in a dialogue designed to provide strategic reassurance regarding U.S. intentions toward the Korean peninsula, with the objective of expanding the level and scope of Sino-U.S. policy coordination toward North Korea.

- Emphasize to China that because North Korea is the only state to have joined and then walked away from the NPT, it will be treated as the prime suspect and target of retaliation in the event of any potential act of nuclear terrorism conducted by nonstate actors.

- Work with China to augment its export control regime and strengthen efforts to freeze financial transfers from North Korean companies suspected of exporting nuclear- or missile-related materials.

- Work with China to promote the Six Party Talks as the premier venue for negotiating the denuclearization of the Korean peninsula.

U.S.-JAPAN COOPERATION

The United States should emphasize the importance of Japan's active involvement as part of its approach to regional cohesion. The Task Force finds that the United States should continue to closely coordinate North Korea policy with Japan through bilateral alliance talks.

- An objective of talks should be to maintain alliance reassurance by closely coordinating North Korea policy, including reiterating U.S. commitments to extended deterrence to reassure Japan that U.S. security assurances are credible, even against the threat of a nuclear attack on Japan.

- The United States and Japan should continue to work together on missile defense to counter North Korea's missile capabilities and on diplomatic measures in support of negotiations with North Korea to put a moratorium on North Korean missile testing back into place.

- The United States should closely coordinate with Japan in advance of any bilateral missile talks with North Korea to ensure that Tokyo's concerns are fully reflected. In addition, Tokyo might consider adding North Korea's midrange missiles to its agenda for bilateral talks with Pyongyang on the premise that North Korea's Rodongs are the most serious threat to Japan.

- U.S.-Japan-ROK policy consultations should be strengthened along the lines of the Trilateral Coordination and Oversight Group (TCOG), a high-level consultative body established by the three countries in the late 1990s that actively coordinated policies toward North Korea until 2002.

- Japan should pursue North Korea's denuclearization as well as resolve the abductee issue on the basis of the 2002 Pyongyang Declaration between North Korea and Japan.

U.S.-ROK ALLIANCE

Alongside the U.S.-Japan alliance, the U.S.-ROK alliance has played a critical role in securing stability in Northeast Asia for more than five decades. The Task Force finds that the June 2009 U.S.-ROK Joint Vision Statement constitutes a valuable foundation for U.S.-ROK cooperation that should be implemented fully to address both peninsular and global challenges. A closer alliance would serve as a platform for South Korea's development of an effective regional diplomacy with Japan and China while also supporting Lee's vision of a "global Korea."

PURSUE CONDITIONS-BASED APPROACH
TO OPERATIONAL CONTROL TRANSFER

The Task Force approves of the agreement to revise OPCON arrangements and institute a new system for coordination with the USFK. It has proceeded smoothly thus far, but new political developments, including the March 2010 sinking of South Korea's *Cheonan* corvette in disputed waters near North Korea, have raised questions regarding whether the timing of the transfer might be delayed from the April 2012 target.

- The Task Force recommends that the two presidents review the progress to date in preparing for revised OPCON arrangements (through which the military commanders will independently coordinate with each other to achieve shared military objectives, rather than pursuing operations under a combined command) based on a technical evaluation of the readiness of the two sides to adopt separate OPCON arrangements. Such an evaluation should occur at least one year before revised OPCON arrangements are implemented, that is, in April 2011.

– If progress to date leads to doubts about the capacity of the two sides to carry out the new arrangements, the two leaders should agree on a revised timetable and order concrete steps necessary to implement it.

RATIFY U.S.-KOREA FREE TRADE AGREEMENT

The Task Force recommends that the Obama administration and Congress take steps to secure ratification of the KORUS FTA at the earliest politically feasible opportunity, ideally just after the U.S. midterm elections. The KORUS FTA is a valuable instrument to bolster U.S.-ROK political and security cooperation and lower barriers to the entry of American products and services in the Korean market. In addition, the KORUS FTA is a net job creator; there is no low-priced Korean labor pool to undercut American jobs, Korean environmental standards are comparable to American environmental standards, and passage of the KORUS FTA will allow American businesses to stay even with European businesses that will shortly enjoy the benefits of the recently negotiated Korea-EU FTA.

The case for ratification of the KORUS FTA is based on the following premises:

– A bilateral FTA would be a high-profile symbol of the bond between the United States and the ROK and would show that the United States remains committed to deepening its engagement in East Asia.

– Ratification would help transform the South Korean economy and cement Korea's position as a regional economic hub, thereby increasing its ability to influence events on the Korean peninsula and in Northeast Asia.

– Ratification would enable the United States to set a standard for trade agreements in Asia beyond their use in public diplomacy or for political purposes.

– The U.S.-ROK economic relationship should be cultivated as a counterweight to the expansion of China's regional economic importance, especially among China's immediate neighbors. Thus, an economic agreement with South Korea carries a strategic message that the United States supports efforts to ensure that South Korea is not overly dependent on China.

Additional and Dissenting Views

I do not subscribe to the view that U.S. policy recommendations as laid out in the report should be prioritized in linear fashion. Proliferation is undeniably a near-term security threat, but explicit rhetorical prioritization of this concern does little to enhance the counterproliferation effort, yet creates mistaken impressions among regional players that we have resigned to containing a nuclear North Korea. Rather than linear priorities, these policies should be pursued on parallel and overlapping tracks.

Victor D. Cha

The Korea Task Force's recommendation for a policy of rollback to confront the North Korean government's nuclear ambitions sounds attractive, but only in theory. In practice, it amounts to a continuation of the failed carrot-and-stick approach to denuclearization through international engagement with Pyongyang that has been attempted already for nearly two decades.

Suffice it to say that over the most recent experiment in engaging North Korea (through Six Party Talks), the DPRK has gone from hinting that it is developing a "war deterrent" to stating that this deterrent is in fact a nuclear arsenal, to testing two atomic weapons, and to insisting that it will not give up its nuclear option "under any circumstances."

The sorry history of nuclear negotiations with the DPRK demonstrates that the international community has absolutely no reason to assume the current North Korean regime will actually denuclearize voluntarily—no matter what blandishments Washington and others proffer or what penalties are threatened. Pyongyang regards its nuclear potential as a vital national interest—and governments do not negotiate vital national interests away.

In essence, the North Korean nuclear problem is the North Korean regime. A nonnuclear North Korea will be possible only under a different government in Pyongyang. This is a highly unpleasant reality. But unless we recognize that reality—rather than imagining Pyongyang as the negotiating partner we wish it to be—continuing the current course can only make for a more dangerous future for the United States and its Asian allies.

Nicholas Eberstadt

After the attack on the *Cheonan*, the first priority in U.S. and ROK policy must be to reestablish deterrence and dissuasion vis-à-vis the DPRK. For this reason, wartime OPCON should be delayed based on the Task Force recommendation that the decision on the timing of the transfer be conditions based. Enhancements of bilateral U.S.-ROK and trilateral U.S.-ROK-Japan security cooperation will also be necessary. Careful thought must also be given to the timing of U.S. and ROK reengagement in the six-party process.

Michael J. Green

Rollback is an unfortunate choice of terms, and is not a strategy but an objective—to denuclearize the peninsula and stop nuclear and missile proliferation. The favored strategy correctly combines strengthening defensive sanctions, seeking to restart the Six Party Talks, offering appropriate inducements, and undertaking economic, social, cultural, and humanitarian engagement. The report wrongly suggests that these policy measures need to be rank ordered, when they should be undertaken in combination. Engagement is a crucial long-run element of any strategy toward North Korea if we are to gradually transform its economy and society and thereby improve the welfare of its people and change its stance toward the world. The report includes mention of a preemptive attack on missile facilities as part of the manage and contain approach, and considers rollback an extension and strengthening of manage and contain. We reject this option as unnecessary and excessively risky.

Stephan Haggard
Susan L. Shirk

We must not seek agreements with North Korea because it does not keep agreements. At least seven agreements with the United States have been broken: the armistice agreement, the North-South Communiqué of 1972, two North-South agreements of 1992, the Agreed Framework of 1994, the Communiqué of the North-South Summit of 2000, and the Nonproliferation Treaty, human right agreements, and others. It is hard to find an agreement that North Korea has kept.

Denuclearization is our key objective for North Korea. But there will be no denuclearization without regime change.

The Task Force report is ambiguous about regime change: it asserts that North Korea's neighbors want a stable transition to a new leadership. Yet a nuclear North Korea constantly creates instability with its nuclear activities. Hence, we do not want a politically "stable" North Korea with nuclear weapons. We have successfully used regime change for Saddam Hussein's regime in Iraq.

However, we should prepare cooperation with China for a North Korean regime collapse. The illness of Kim Jong-il and his quirky succession plans make regime collapse likely. The United States should assure China that American military forces would not go north of the demilitarized żone, and that they would be withdrawn from South Korea if China did not move military forces into North Korea, except to secure nuclear weapons. Such a preparation for regime collapse might also make China more tolerant if we initiate and succeed with regime change.

Fred C. Iklé

I like very much the thrust of this report, and greatly respect the ideas and experience of the Task Force leaders, but I do have two issues requiring dissent. First, even though it may be unrealistic at the moment, I believe a truly comprehensive agenda with North Korea must also include the promotion of economic reform within the DPRK, inspired in part by the Vietnam and China models. This can work only if Pyongyang plays ball, of course, and that seems out of the question at the moment. But the fact remains that such reform is needed, and is integral to any truly viable path for changing the basic nature of the North Korean regime as well as its relationship with the outside world. Second, I oppose OPCON transfer categorically. In fact, I believe it is a misnomer; current plans would not achieve OPCON transfer so much as the bifurcation of operational control between U.S. and ROK forces on the peninsula. I fear this could significantly complicate wartime operations, under either 5027 or 5029 scenarios (that is, classic warfighting, or North Korean collapse/stabilization operations) and thereby weaken deterrence as well. Unity of command is such a central principle to successful military operations that I cannot personally support the decision to dismantle it within the U.S.-ROK alliance. Delaying the transfer beyond 2012, as the Task Force is prepared to countenance, might mitigate the problem but does not solve it.

Michael O'Hanlon

While I believe that the Task Force has correctly identified the four major policy options, I do not share the belief that rollback is the preferable option. The loss of leverage after the North exploded two nuclear devices, plus the unwillingness of some regional players to endorse and, more importantly, enforce tough sanctions, makes rollback very unlikely to be viable. The current policy, which the Task Force has labeled as manage and contain while remaining publicly committed to rollback, strikes me as the best we're going to get until regime change comes to North Korea. Rather than describe current policy as halfhearted, I view it as pragmatic and prudent. Without raising either expectations or tensions it permits the U.S. administration to seek progress on some of the other areas highlighted in the report, including contingency planning and bilateral missile negotiations.

Stanley Owen Roth

I wish to highlight a major and a minor point in this otherwise excellent report. First and foremost, if the Task Force is correct that "it is a top priority in U.S.-China relations to make progress in bringing North Korea back to the path of denuclearization"—and I believe it is—then Beijing's sustained life support for the Kim regime is clearly the key to the rollback and the regime change options. I doubt that "a dialogue designed to provide strategic reassurance" will convince China's leaders to cut the lifeline to their client state to the east. Instead, diplomatic, economic, and military pressure of the highest order, and on a multilateral basis, will be required.

Second (and minor) is the timing of OPCON transfer to the Republic of Korea. The report suggests flexibility in this. To the contrary, I believe a firm mutual deadline is essential to ensure that Seoul acquires the military capabilities and political confidence to assume prime responsibility for the defense of the South.

James J. Shinn

Endnotes

1. See special online Appendix: September 19, 2005, Six Party Joint Statement, http://www.cfr.org/korea_task_force.
2. See previous CFR-sponsored Independent Task Force reports, http://www.cfr.org/publication/publication_list.html?type=task_force_report.
3. "DPRK Foreign Ministry's Spokesman Dismisses U.S. Wrong Assertion," *Korean Central News Agency*, January 17, 2009.
4. "Remarks by President Barack Obama," Hradcany Square, Prague, Czech Republic, April 5, 2009, http://www.whitehouse.gov/the_press_office/Remarks-By-President-Barack-Obama-In-Prague-As-Delivered/.
5. "Security Council Condemns Launch by Democratic People's Republic of Korea, Agrees to Adjust Travel Ban, Assets Freeze, Arms Embargo Imposed in 2006," Security Council news release SC/9634, April 13, 2009, http://www.un.org/News/Press/docs/2009/sc9634.doc.htm.
6. "DPRK Foreign Ministry Vehemently Refutes UNSC's 'Presidential Statement,'" *Korean Central News Agency*, April 14, 2009.
7. "Security Council, Acting Unanimously, Condemns in Strongest Terms Democratic People's Republic of Korea Nuclear Test, Toughens Sanctions," Security Council news release SC/9679, June 12, 2009, http://www.un.org/News/Press/docs/2009/sc9679.doc.htm.
8. Through the end of 2009, in a half-dozen cases shipments of weapons from North Korea have been inspected in port or interdicted in accordance with the UN resolution, which imposes an asset freeze and travel ban against transfer of assets or resources that could contribute to North Korea's nuclear or missile programs, and calls on member states to not provide financial assistance, grants, or liens to North Korea for any purpose other than to meet civilian humanitarian and development needs.
9. Philip W. Yun, "The North Korean Nuclear Weapons Problem: Why Regime Change Through Coercion Won't Work," in Philip W. Yun and Gi-Wook Shin, eds., *North Korea: 2005 and Beyond* (Washington, DC: Shorenstein APARC and Brookings Institution Press, 2006), pp. 211–50.
10. *Nuclear Posture Review Report* (Washington, DC: U.S. Department of Defense, April 2010), http://www.defense.gov/npr/docs/2010%20nuclear%20posture%20review%20report.pdf.
11. "Remarks by President Obama and President Lee Myung-bak of the Republic of Korea in the Joint Press Availability," White House Office of Press Secretary, June 16, 2009, http://www.whitehouse.gov/the_press_office/Remarks-by-President-Obama-and-President-Lee-of-the-Republic-of-Korea-in-Joint-Press-Availability; "Remarks by the President at the Acceptance of the Nobel Peace Prize," White House Office of the Press Secretary, December 10, 2009, http://www.whitehouse.gov/the-press-office/remarks-president-acceptance-nobel-peace-prize.

12. Secretary of Defense Robert M. Gates, touring an antimissile site in Alaska, quoted in "U.S. Weighs Intercepting North Korean Shipments," *New York Times*, June 7, 2009, http://www.nytimes.com/2009/06/08/world/asia/08korea.html.
13. Hillary Rodham Clinton, "Remarks at the United States Institute of Peace," Washington, DC, October 21, 2009, http://www.state.gov/secretary/rm/2009a/10/130806.htm.
14. Chang Won Lim, "Envoy Says U.S., DPRK Agree on Need to Resume Nuclear Disarmament Negotiations," *Agence France Press*, December 10, 2009.
15. For more information on the status and scope of North Korea's nuclear program, see Siegfried S. Hecker, "Lessons Learned from the North Korean Crises," Stanford University Center for International Security and Cooperation, 2010, http://www.cisac.stanford.edu/publications/lessons_learned_from_the_North_Korean_crises.
16. *Ballistic Missile Defense Review Report* (Washington, DC: U.S. Department of Defense, February 2010).
17. Clinton, "Remarks at the United States Institute of Peace."
18. Ashton B. Carter and William J. Perry, "If Necessary, Strike and Destroy: North Korea Cannot Be Allowed to Test This Missile," *Washington Post*, June 22, 2006; Charles L. "Jack" Pritchard, "No, Don't Blow It Up: A Saner Approach to North Korea's Missile Test," *Washington Post*, June 23, 2006.
19. The Task Force is indebted to Siegfried S. Hecker for his explication of the three *nos*.
20. See Andrei Lankov, "The North Korean Paradox and the Subversive Truth," AEI *Asian Outlook* No. 1, March 2009, http://www.aei.org/outlook/100014.
21. See Charles Kartman and Susan Shirk, "North Korea Inside Out: The Case for Economic Engagement" (New York and La Jolla: Asia Society and University of California Institute on Global Conflict and Cooperation, 2009), http://www.asiasociety.org/policy-politics/international-relations/us-asia/north-korea-inside-out.
22. See Bradley O. Babson, "Transformation and Modernization of North Korea: Implications for Future Engagement" (project paper, National Committee for North Korea, October 1, 2009), http://www.ncnk.org/resources/publications/Transformation_and_Modernization_of_North%20Korea.pdf.
23. Scott Snyder, *China's Rise and the Two Koreas: Politics, Economics, Security* (Boulder, CO: Lynne Rienner Publishers, 2009).
24. "China criticizes Japan over talk of preemptive strike on N. Korea," *Yonhap*, July 13, 2006.
25. Author conversations in Beijing, July 2007.
26. Seung-ho Joo, "Russia and the North Korean Nuclear Crisis," in Seung-ho Joo and Tae-hwan Kwak, eds., *North Korea's Second Nuclear Crisis and Northeast Asian Security* (Aldershot, UK: Ashgate, 2007), pp. 133–50.
27. "Remarks of Vice President Biden at National Defense University," White House Office of the Vice President, February 18, 2010, http://www.whitehouse.gov/the-press-office/remarks-vice-president-biden-national-defense-university.
28. President Lee Myung-bak's inaugural address, "Together We Shall Open A Road to Advancement," Seoul, South Korea, February 25, 2008, http://www.korea.net/news/Issues/issueDetailView.asp?board_no=18994.
29. See Paul B. Stares and Joel S. Wit, *Preparing for Sudden Change in North Korea* (New York: Council on Foreign Relations Press, 2009).
30. Michael Finnegan, "Preparing for the Inevitable in North Korea," PacNet No. 28B (Honolulu, HI: Pacific Forum CSIS, April 28, 2009), http://csis.org/files/media/csis/pubs/pac0928b.pdf.
31. Carter and Perry, "If Necessary, Strike and Destroy: North Korea Cannot Be Allowed to Test This Missile"; Pritchard, "No, Don't Blow It Up: A Saner Approach to North Korea's Missile Test."
32. Joseph S. Bermudez Jr., "A History of Ballistic Missile Development in the DPRK,"

Center for Nonproliferation Studies Occasional Paper No. 2 (Monterey, CA: Monterey Institute of International Studies, 1999), http://cns.miis.edu/opapers/op2/op2.pdf.

33. Kim So-hyun, "Worries resurface over N.K.-Iran nuclear deals," *Korea Herald*, March 18, 2010, http://www.koreaherald.co.kr/national/Detail.jsp?newsMLId=20100318000083.

34. Larry Niksch, cited at the conference "Engaging China to Solve the North Korea Problem," CATO Institute, Washington, DC, July 14, 2009.

35. An additional dimension of WMD of concern is North Korea's arsenal of chemical and biological weapons. This aspect of WMD will have to be addressed either as a dimension of North Korea's nuclear program or as a special subject that might be attached to conventional arms reductions.

36. See Appendix: Resolution 1874.

37. David Hawk, *The Hidden Gulag: Exposing North Korea's Prison Camps* (Washington, DC: Committee for Human Rights in North Korea, 2003), http://www.hrnk.org/download/The Hidden Gulag.pdf.

38. "Democratic People's Republic of Korea," in *2010 Index of Economic Freedom* (Washington, DC: Heritage Foundation, 2010), pp. 255–56, http://www.heritage.org/Index/pdf/2010/countries/northkorea.pdf.

39. "Defectors assimilate in S. Korea," Associated Press, July 8, 2009.

40. Mark E. Manyin and Mary Beth Nikitin, "Foreign Assistance to North Korea," CRS Report R40095 (Washington, DC: Congressional Research Service, September 9, 2009), http://www.fas.org/sgp/crs/row/R40095.pdf.

41. Stephan Haggard, Marcus Noland, and Erik Weeks, "North Korea on the Precipice of Famine," Peterson Institute Policy Brief PB08-6 (Washington, DC: Peterson Institute for International Economics, May 2008), http://www.iie.com/publications/pb/pb08-6.pdf.

42. See Manyin and Nikitin, "Foreign Assistance to North Korea."

43. See Appendix: June 2009 U.S.-ROK Joint Vision Statement.

44. The Joint Vision Statement is available at http://www.whitehouse.gov/the_press_office/Joint-vision-for-the-alliance-of-the-United-States-of-America-and-the-Republic-of-Korea.

45. "The 39th Security Consultative Meeting Joint Communiqué," news release 1290-07, November 7, 2007, http://www.defense.gov/news/Nov2007/39THSCMJointCommunique.pdf.

46. Jeffrey Schott, "Implementing the KORUS FTA: Key Challenges and Policy Proposals," in L. Gordon Flake and Park Ro-byug, eds., *Understanding New Political Realities in Seoul: Working Toward a Common Approach to Strengthen U.S.-Korean Relations* (Washington, DC: Maureen and Mike Mansfield Foundation, 2008).

47. See, for example, Donald Kirk, "South Korean beef overcooked," *Asia Times*, May 6, 2008, http://www.atimes.com/atimes/Korea/JE06Dg01.html.

48. William H. Cooper, Mark E. Manyin, Remy Jurenas, and Michaela D. Platzer, "The Proposed U.S.-South Korea Free Trade Agreement (KORUS FTA): Provisions and Implications," CRS Report RL34330 (Washington, DC: Congressional Research Service, June 17, 2009), http://www.fas.org/sgp/crs/row/RL34330.pdf.

49. Kevin Nealer, "Reimagining Obama Trade Policy," PacNet No. 43 (Honolulu, HI: Pacific Forum CSIS, June 11, 2009), http://csis.org/files/publication/pac0943.pdf.

50. "USTR Releases Preliminary Analysis of KOREA-EU Free Trade Agreement," press release, October 21, 2009, http://www.ustr.gov/about-us/press-office/press-releases/2009/october/ustr-releases-preliminary-analysis-korea-eu-free-t.

51. Troy Stangarone, "Korea-EU FTA Represents a Challenge for the United States," KEIA *Insight*, November 2009, http://www.keia.org/Publications/Insight/2009/09November.pdf.

52. U.S. International Trade Commission, *U.S.-Korea Free Trade Agreement: Potential Economy-wide and Selected Sectoral Effects*, USITC Publication 3949 (Washington, DC: U.S. International Trade Commission, 2007), http://www.usitc.gov/publications/332/pub3949.pdf.

53. See Karin Lee, "Working at the People-to-People Level: Recommendations for United States Government Involvement; Humanitarian Assistance, Development Assistance, and Exchange Programs with the Democratic People's Republic of Korea" (project paper, National Committee for North Korea, 2009), http://www.ncnk.org/resources/publications/Karin_Lee_Humanitarian_Recommendations_10-09.pdf.

Task Force Members

Task Force members are asked to join a consensus signifying that they endorse "the general policy thrust and judgments reached by the group, though not necessarily every finding and recommendation." They participate in the Task Force in their individual, not their institutional, capacities.

Michael R. Auslin is a resident scholar in foreign and defense policy studies and director of Japan studies at the American Enterprise Institute for Public Policy Research. Auslin specializes in U.S.-Asia relations, U.S. security policy, and Asian maritime security. Auslin was an associate professor of history at Yale University and senior research fellow at Yale's MacMillan Center for International and Area Studies prior to joining AEI. He has been named a Young Global Leader by the World Economic Forum, a Marshall memorial fellow by the German Marshall Fund, an Asia 21 fellow by the Asia Society, and a Fulbright and Japan Foundation scholar. His writings include the award-winning book *Negotiating with Imperialism: The Unequal Treaties and the Culture of Japanese Diplomacy* and the report *Securing Freedom: The U.S.-Japanese Alliance in a New Era*. His new history of U.S.-Japan relations will be published in 2011. A columnist for the *Wall Street Journal*, he appears regularly in U.S. and foreign media commenting on current Asia issues. Auslin graduated with honors from Georgetown University's School of Foreign Service and was awarded a PhD in history from the University of Illinois at Urbana-Champaign.

Douglas K. Bereuter is the president and CEO of the Asia Foundation, headquartered in San Francisco. Immediately before this position he served for twenty-six years in the U.S. House of Representatives. He served for twenty years on the House Foreign Affairs Committee, was its vice chairman for six years, chaired the Asia-Pacific subcommittee for the six-year maximum, chaired the Europe subcommittee immediately before leaving Congress, served on the Human Rights subcommittee for six years, and had a long tenure on the Economic Policy and Trade subcommittee. Bereuter was a longtime member of the House delegation to the NATO Parliamentary Assembly, and served as its president. He also served nearly ten years on the House Permanent Select Committee on Intelligence, retiring as its vice chairman. Bereuter is a member of the Council on Foreign Relations and the Pacific Council on International Policy.

Victor D. Cha holds the D. S. Song chair in government and Asian studies at Georgetown University. He is concurrently a senior adviser and the Korea chair at the Center for Strategic and International Studies. Cha is a former two-time Fulbright scholar, John M. Olin fellow at Harvard, and Hoover national fellow at Stanford University. He has authored three books, including *Nuclear North Korea* with David Kang. Cha served on the National Security Council staff from 2004 to 2007 and was the U.S. deputy head of delegation for the Six Party Talks.

Charles B. Curtis is president emeritus and board member of the Nuclear Threat Initiative and senior adviser at the Center for Strategic and International Studies. Curtis served for nine years as president and chief executive officer of NTI. Before joining NTI, Curtis served as the executive vice president and chief operating officer of the United Nations Foundation and was a partner in Hogan & Hartson, a Washington, DC–based law firm with domestic and international offices. Curtis served as undersecretary and, later, deputy secretary of the U.S. Department of Energy from February 1994 to May 1997. He was chief operating officer of the department and, among other duties, had direct programmatic responsibility for all of the department's energy, science, technology, and national security programs. Curtis is a lawyer with over fifteen years' practice experience and more than eighteen years in government service. He was a founding partner of the Washington, DC, law firm Van Ness Feldman. Curtis served as chairman of the Federal Energy Regulatory Commission from 1977 to 1981 and has held positions on the staff of the U.S. House of Representatives, the U.S. Department of the Treasury, and the Securities and Exchange Commission. He is a current member of the Council on Foreign Relations.

Nicholas Eberstadt holds the Henry Wendt chair in political economy at the American Enterprise Institute and is senior adviser to the National Bureau of Asian Research. He is, among else, a member of the advisory council for the Korea Economic Institute and of the board of directors for the U.S. Committee for Human Rights in North Korea. He has written extensively on issues in demography, development, and international security, and has published hundreds of articles or studies and written or coauthored nearly twenty books, monographs, or edited volumes. His most recent books on North Korea are *The North Korean Economy: Between Crisis and Catastrophe* and *Policy and Economic Performance in Divided Korea during the Cold War Era: 1945–1991*. Eberstadt earned his AB, MPA, and PhD from Harvard University, and his MSc from the London School of Economics.

Robert L. Gallucci became president of the John D. and Catherine T. MacArthur Foundation on July 1, 2009. Previously, he served for thirteen years as dean of Georgetown University's Edmund A. Walsh School of Foreign Service. He completed twenty-one years of government service, serving since August 1994 with the U.S. Department of State as ambassador at large. In March 1998, the Department of State announced his appointment as special envoy to deal with the threat posed by the proliferation of ballistic missiles and weapons of mass destruction. He held this position, concurrent with his appointment as dean, until January 2001. Gallucci earned a bachelor's degree from the State University of New York at Stony Brook, followed by a master's and doctorate in politics from Brandeis University. Before joining the State Department, he taught at Swarthmore College, the Johns Hopkins School of Advanced International Studies, and Georgetown University. He has authored a number of publications on political-military issues, including *Neither Peace Nor Honor: The Politics of American Military Policy in Vietnam* and *Going Critical: The First North Korean Nuclear Crisis* with Joel S. Wit and Daniel Poneman. For *Going Critical*, he was the recipient of the 2005 Douglas Dillon Award given by the American Academy of Diplomacy for a book of distinction in the practice of diplomacy.

Michael J. Green is senior adviser and Japan chair at the Center for Strategic and International Studies and associate professor at the Edmund

A. Walsh School of Foreign Service at Georgetown University. He served on the National Security Council staff from 2001 through 2005 as director for Asian affairs and then special assistant to the president for national security affairs and senior director for Asian affairs. From 1997 to 2001 he was Olin senior fellow for Asian security studies at the Council on Foreign Relations, where he also directed CFR's Independent Task Force on Korea. He has also held positions at the Institute for Defense Analyses and the Office of the Secretary of Defense, and on the faculty of the Johns Hopkins School of Advanced International Studies, where he completed his doctoral work. He is vice chair of the congressionally mandated U.S.-Japan Friendship Commission, a member of the Council on Foreign Relations and the Aspen Strategy Group, and he sits on the advisory boards of the Center for a New American Security, Peacewinds, and the Australia-America Leadership Dialogue.

Stephan Haggard is the Lawrence and Sallye Krause professor at the Graduate School of International Relations and Pacific Studies, University of California, San Diego, and director of the Korea-Pacific program there. He is the author, with Marcus Noland, of *Famine in North Korea: Markets, Aid, and Reform* and *Witness to Transformation: Refugee Insights on North Korea*.

Siegfried S. Hecker is codirector of the Stanford University Center for International Security and Cooperation, senior fellow of the Freeman Spogli Institute for International Studies, and research professor in the department of management science and engineering. He is also director emeritus at the Los Alamos National Laboratory, where he served as director from 1986 to 1997 and as senior fellow until July 2005. He received his BS, MS, and PhD degrees in metallurgy from Case Western Reserve University. His current professional interests include plutonium research, nuclear weapons policy, cooperative nuclear threat reduction with the Russian nuclear complex, and global nonproliferation and counterterrorism. Hecker is a member of the National Academy of Engineering and a foreign member of the Russian Academy of Sciences. He is also a member of the Council on Foreign Relations, fellow of the American Physical Society, the American Academy of Arts and Sciences, the American Association for the Advancement of Science, the Metallurgical Society, and ASM International, and an honorary member of the American Ceramics

Society. Among other awards, he received the Presidential Enrico Fermi Award, the Los Alamos National Laboratory Medal, the U.S. Department of Energy's E.O. Lawrence Award, and the American Nuclear Society Seaborg Award.

Fred C. Iklé is a distinguished scholar at the Center for Strategic and International Studies. He is a member of the Defense Policy Board, a governor of the Smith Richardson Foundation, and a director of the U.S. Committee for Human Rights in North Korea. Iklé was undersecretary of defense for policy during the first and second Reagan administrations. From 1979 to 1980, he served as coordinator of Governor Ronald Reagan's foreign policy advisers. From 1973 to 1977, he served presidents Nixon and Ford as director of the U.S. Arms Control and Disarmament Agency. From 1964 to 1967, Iklé was a professor of political science at the Massachusetts Institute of Technology. He has held positions with the RAND Corporation and the Bureau of Applied Social Research at Columbia University. His many publications include *Annihilation from Within, Every War Must End,* and *How Nations Negotiate.* In 1987, Iklé received the highest civilian award of the Department of Defense, the Distinguished Public Service Medal, and in 1988 was awarded the Bronze Palm.

Charles Jones joined Lockheed Martin in June 2005, where he is currently the director for corporate international business development in South and Central Asia. Just prior to joining Lockheed Martin, Jones served as the deputy director of the Pentagon's tsunami relief task force. From January 2004 to January 2005, he served as director for Asia on the National Security Council with responsibility for Japan, Australia, New Zealand, North Korea, and the Republic of Korea (ROK). A career Department of Defense civil servant, he came to the National Security Council from the Office of the Secretary of Defense, where he was country director for Korea, responsible for the realignment of U.S. forces based in the ROK. Prior to that assignment, Jones was the senior policy and plans analyst for Northeast Asia in the Defense Prisoner of War/Missing Personnel Office, where he participated in negotiations for access by U.S. teams looking for the remains of American military personnel in North Korea. In that capacity, he traveled to North Korea on several occasions, which included a monthlong tour as liaison officer in Pyongyang for the recovery teams.

William J. Lennox Jr. of Alexandria, Virginia, retired in June 2006 after a thirty-five-year career in the U.S. Army. He retired as the fifty-sixth superintendent of the U.S. Military Academy. His service included commands at every level of field artillery. His staff positions included tours as a White House fellow and as a special assistant to the secretary of the army. He also served as assistant chief of staff, CJ-3, Combined Forces Command/United States Forces Korea and deputy commanding general, Eighth U.S. Army, and as the army's chief of legislative liaison. In addition to his BS from the U.S. Military Academy, General Lennox holds an MA and a PhD in literature from Princeton University. His military education includes the Senior Service College fellowship at Harvard University. General Lennox's awards include the Defense Distinguished Service Medal, the Distinguished Service Medal with Oak Leaf Cluster, the French Legion of Honor, and the Korean Order of Military Merit, Inheon Medal. General Lennox currently serves as senior vice president, Washington, for Goodrich Corporation, a Fortune 500 aerospace firm.

Marcus Noland is deputy director and senior fellow at the Peter G. Peterson Institute for International Economics and a senior fellow at the East-West Center. He was a senior economist at the Council of Economic Advisers in the Executive Office of the President of the United States, and has held research or teaching positions at Yale University, the Johns Hopkins University, the University of Southern California, Tokyo University, Saitama University (now the National Graduate Institute for Policy Studies), the University of Ghana, and the Korea Development Institute. Noland has authored, coauthored, or edited numerous books including *Korea After Kim Jong-il, Economic Integration of the Korean Peninsula,* and *Famine in North Korea: Markets, Aid, and Reform* (with Stephan Haggard). His book *Avoiding the Apocalypse: The Future of the Two Koreas* won the prestigious Ohira Memorial Prize. In addition to these books he has written many scholarly articles on international economics, U.S. trade policy, and the economies of the Asia-Pacific region. He has served as an occasional consultant to organizations such as the World Bank and the National Intelligence Council, and has testified before the U.S. Congress on numerous occasions.

Don Oberdorfer is a distinguished journalist in residence and adjunct professor of international relations at the Johns Hopkins School of

Advanced International Studies. In September 2006, he was named chairman of the U.S.-Korea Institute at SAIS. Oberdorfer was a journalist for thirty-eight years, twenty-five of them for the *Washington Post*. He has also reported for the *Charlotte Observer*, the *Saturday Evening Post*, and Knight Newspapers. His work has won numerous awards, including the National Press Club's Edwin M. Hood Award for diplomatic correspondence (1981, 1988) and Georgetown University's annual Edward Weintal Prize for diplomatic reporting (1982, 1993). He retired from journalism in 1993. From 1994 to 1996 Oberdorfer served as president of Overseas Writers, and from 1986 to 1989 he chaired the advisory committee of the Washington Center of the Asia Society. He is a member of the Asia Society and the Council on Foreign Relations, and currently is program chair of the Washington Institute on Foreign Affairs. Oberdorfer graduated from Princeton University in 1952 and returned as a visiting professor in 1977, 1982, and 1986. In 1996, Princeton bestowed on him its Woodrow Wilson Award, given annually to an alumnus for exemplary service to the nation.

Michael O'Hanlon is a senior fellow in foreign policy at the Brookings Institution, where he specializes in U.S. defense strategy, the use of military force, homeland security, and American foreign policy. He is also director of research in the foreign policy program at Brookings. A visiting lecturer at Princeton University and adjunct professor at Johns Hopkins University, O'Hanlon is a member of the International Institute for Strategic Studies and the Council on Foreign Relations. He was a member of the secretary of state's International Security Advisory Board in 2009 and an informal adviser to General David H. Petraeus during his 2008–2009 CENTCOM review of Mideast security strategy.

Jonathan D. Pollack is professor of Asian and Pacific Studies and chairman of the Asia-Pacific Studies Group at the Naval War College. He is also a nonresident senior fellow at the Brookings Institution and a research associate in the National Asia Research Program of the National Bureau of Asian Research and the Woodrow Wilson International Center for Scholars. Prior to joining the War College faculty, he was affiliated with the RAND Corporation, where he served in various research and senior management capacities. He has taught at Brandeis University, the RAND Graduate School of Policy Studies, and UCLA. A specialist on East Asian international politics and security, he has published extensively on Chinese political-military strategy, U.S.-China relations, the political and security dynamics of the Korean Peninsula, and U.S. strategy and policy in Asia and the Pacific. He is author of, most recently, the forthcoming book *No Exit: North Korea, Nuclear Weapons, and International Security.*

Charles L. Pritchard is the president of the Korea Economic Institute in Washington, DC. Prior to joining KEI, he was a visiting fellow at the Brookings Institution in Washington, DC, from September 2003 until February 2006. He is the author of *Failed Diplomacy: The Tragic Story of How North Korea Got the Bomb.* Pritchard served as ambassador and special envoy for negotiations with the Democratic People's Republic of Korea and as U.S. representative to the Korean Peninsula Energy Development Organization in the administration of President George W. Bush from April 2001 until September 2003. Previously, he served as special assistant to the president for national security affairs and as senior director for Asian affairs in the administration of President William J. Clinton. Ambassador Pritchard obtained his BA in political science from Mercer University in Georgia and his MA in international studies from the University of Hawaii. He is also a graduate of the Japan National Institute for Defense Studies, Class 40. Pritchard retired from the U.S. Army as a colonel after twenty-eight years of service. He is the recipient of the Defense Distinguished Service Medal.

Evans J.R. Revere is senior director with the Albright Stonebridge Group, where he advises clients on entry and growth strategies throughout the Asia-Pacific region, with a specific focus on Korea, China, and Japan. Previously, he was president/CEO of the Korea Society, the leading U.S. private, nonprofit organization devoted to improving U.S.-Korea relations. In 2007, he retired after a long and distinguished career as an American diplomat and one of the Department of State's top Asia experts. An expert on Korea, Japan, and China, his diplomatic career included service as the principal deputy assistant secretary of state for East Asian and Pacific affairs and as deputy chief of mission and charge d'affaires of the U.S. embassy in Seoul. He has extensive experience in negotiations with the DPRK. He is fluent in Korean, Japanese, and Chinese, and is a member of the Council on Foreign Relations.

Stanley Owen Roth is vice president of international government relations for the Boeing Company. In this role, he amalgamates country and regional issues pertinent to Boeing's interests into a comprehensive view of international government affairs, and works closely with Boeing government operations to create an integrated view of U.S. and global government issues and developments. Before this appointment, he was Boeing vice president of international relations, Asia. Prior to joining Boeing in May 2001, Roth served as assistant secretary of state for Asian and Pacific affairs from August 1997 until January 2001. He was the senior government official responsible, on a daily basis, for the formulation and execution of U.S. policy for Northeast and Southeast Asia. Before this, Roth served as director of research and studies at the U.S. Institute of Peace from January 1996 through June 1997. In June 1996, while at the institute, he was asked to serve as an administration envoy to six Asian countries concerning Myanmar. Before joining the institute, Roth served as special assistant to the president and senior director for Asian affairs at the National Security Council, beginning in March 1994. Roth is a member of the Council on Foreign Relations and the Asia Society.

James J. Shinn teaches at Princeton University's engineering department. From 2007 to 2008, he served as assistant secretary for Asia in the Department of Defense, where his area of policy responsibility ranged from Herat to Honolulu. Before coming to the Pentagon, he was the national intelligence officer for East Asia, first at the Central Intelligence Agency and then for the director of National Intelligence, from 2003 to 2006. He was the senior fellow for Asia at the Council on Foreign Relations from 1993 to 1996. Shinn served in the East Asia Bureau of the State Department from 1976 to 1979 and then spent fifteen years as a manager and entrepreneur in Silicon Valley. He is a cofounder of Dialogic, which went public in 1992. Shinn earned a BA and a PhD from Princeton University and an MBA from Harvard University.

Susan L. Shirk is the director of the University of California Institute on Global Conflict and Cooperation and the Ho Miu Lam professor at the Graduate School of International Relations and Pacific Studies, University of California, San Diego. She was deputy assistant secretary of state for East Asia and the Pacific from 1997 to 2000 and leads the track-two

Northeast Asia Cooperation Dialogue. She is the author of *China: Fragile Superpower* and editor of *Changing Media, Changing China*.

Scott A. Snyder is adjunct senior fellow for Korea studies at the Council on Foreign Relations. Snyder is director of the Center for U.S.-Korea Policy and senior associate of Washington programs in the international relations program of the Asia Foundation and Pacific Forum CSIS. He lived in Seoul, South Korea, as Korea representative of the Asia Foundation from 2000 to 2004. Previously, he served as a program officer in the research and studies program of the U.S. Institute of Peace, and as acting director of the Asia Society's contemporary affairs program. His latest monograph is *China's Rise and the Two Koreas: Economics, Politics, Security*. His publications include *Paved with Good Intentions: The NGO Experience in North Korea*, coedited with L. Gordon Flake, and *Negotiating on the Edge: North Korean Negotiating Behavior*. Snyder received a BA from Rice University and an MA from the Regional Studies–East Asia program at Harvard University. He was the recipient of a Pantech visiting fellowship at Stanford University's Shorenstein Asia-Pacific Research Center (2005–2006), received an Abe fellowship administered by the Social Sciences Research Council (1998–99), and was a Thomas G. Watson fellow at Yonsei University in South Korea (1987–88).

John H. Tilelli Jr. has been a member of the Cypress International team since 2002, where he currently serves as chairman and CEO. He retired in January 2000 from the U.S. Army after more than thirty years of service. His last active duty assignment was as commander in chief of the United Nations Command, Republic of Korea/United States Combined Forces Command/United States Forces Korea. General Tilelli served as president and CEO of USO Worldwide Operations from 2000 to 2002. He commanded the largest standing joint and coalition force in the world, comprising more than 650,000 soldiers, sailors, airmen, and marines. He led the theater's campaign strategy and revitalized Korea's automated command and control and equipment modernization. He served as vice chief of staff of the army and the army's deputy chief of operations. He led the army's vision of the army of the twenty-first century and implemented reforms in acquisition and procurement. He was commander of the 1st Cavalry Division, Fort Hood, Texas. He trained, deployed, and fought with the division in Operation Desert Shield and Desert Storm. General Tilelli graduated in 1963 from Pennsylvania Military College, now Widener University, with a degree in economics. He was awarded a master's degree in administration from Lehigh University. He is a graduate of the U.S. Army War College. He received an honorary doctorate in business management from Widener University and another in law from the University of Maryland.

Task Force Observers

Observers participate in Task Force discussions, but are not asked to join the consensus. They participate in their individual, not institutional, capacities.

Evan A. Feigenbaum is senior fellow for East, Central, and South Asia at the Council on Foreign Relations. From 2001 to 2009, he served at the U.S. Department of State in various capacities: as deputy assistant secretary of state for South Asia, deputy assistant secretary of state for Central Asia, member of the policy planning staff with principal responsibility for East Asia and the Pacific, and as an adviser on China to Deputy Secretary of State Robert B. Zoellick, with whom he worked closely in the development of the U.S.-China senior dialogue. During the intensive final phase of the U.S.-India civil nuclear initiative from July to October 2008, he co-chaired the coordinating team charged with moving the agreement through the International Atomic Energy Agency board of governors and the Nuclear Suppliers Group, and then to Congress, where it became the U.S.-India Nuclear Cooperation Approval and Nonproliferation Enhancement Act. He received the department's Superior Honor Award five times. Before his government service, Feigenbaum worked at Harvard University, where he was lecturer on government in the Faculty of Arts and Sciences, and executive director of the Asia-Pacific Security Initiative and program chair of the Chinese security studies program in the John F. Kennedy School of Government. He received his AB in history from the University of Michigan and his AM and PhD in political science from Stanford University.

Mark Manyin is a specialist in Asian affairs at the Congressional Research Service, a nonpartisan agency that provides information and analysis to members of the U.S. Congress and their staffs. At

CRS, Manyin's general area of expertise is U.S. foreign economic policy toward East Asia, particularly Japan, the Koreas, and Vietnam. He also has tracked the evolution of terrorism in Southeast Asia and the environmental causes of security tensions in Asia. From 2006 to 2008, Manyin served as the head of the CRS's eleven-person Asia section, overseeing research on East, Southeast, and South Asia as well as on Australasia and the Pacific Islands. Prior to joining CRS in 1999, Manyin completed his PhD in Japanese trade policy and negotiating behavior at the Fletcher School of Law and Diplomacy. He has written academic articles on Vietnam and Korea, taught courses in East Asian international relations, and worked as a business consultant.

Sheila A. Smith, an expert on Japanese politics and foreign policy, is senior fellow for Japan studies at the Council on Foreign Relations and directed the CFR Regional Security Architecture for Asia program. Smith joined CFR from the East-West Center in 2007, where she specialized on Asia-Pacific international relations and U.S. policy toward Asia. She was also recently affiliated with Keio University in Tokyo, where she researched and wrote on Japan's foreign policy toward China and the Northeast Asian region on an Abe fellowship. From 2004 to 2007, she directed a multinational research team in a cross-national study of the domestic politics of the U.S. military presence in Japan, South Korea, and the Philippines. Prior to joining the East-West Center, Smith was on the faculty of the Department of International Relations at Boston University (1994–2000) and on the staff of the Social Science Research Council (1992–93). She has been a visiting researcher at two leading Japanese foreign and security policy think tanks, the Japan Institute of International Affairs and the Research Institute for Peace and Security, and at the University of Tokyo and the University of the Ryukyus. Smith earned her MA and PhD degrees in political science at Columbia University.

Paul B. Stares is the General John W. Vessey senior fellow for conflict prevention and director of the Center for Preventive Action at the Council on Foreign Relations. Besides overseeing a series of Council Special Reports on potential sources of instability and strife, he is currently working on a study assessing long-term conflict trends. Prior to joining CFR, Stares was the vice president and director of the Center for Conflict Analysis and Prevention at the United States Institute of Peace.

Stares worked as an associate director and senior research scholar at Stanford University's Center for International Security and Cooperation from 2000 to 2002, was a senior research fellow at the Japan Institute of International Affairs and director of studies at the Japan Center for International Exchange from 1996 to 2000, and was a senior fellow and research associate in the foreign policy studies program at the Brookings Institution from 1984 to 1996. He has also been a NATO fellow and a scholar-in-residence at the MacArthur Foundation's Moscow office. Stares is the author of numerous books and articles, including *Preparing for Sudden Change in North Korea*. He received his MA and PhD from the University of Lancaster, England.

Independent Task Force Reports

Published by the Council on Foreign Relations

U.S. Immigration Policy
Jeb Bush and Thomas F. McLarty III, Chairs; Edward Alden, Project Director
Independent Task Force Report No. 63 (2009)

U.S. Nuclear Weapons Policy
William J. Perry and Brent Scowcroft, Chairs; Charles D. Ferguson, Project Director
Independent Task Force Report No. 62 (2009)

Confronting Climate Change: A Strategy for U.S. Foreign Policy
George E. Pataki and Thomas J. Vilsack, Chairs; Michael A. Levi, Project Director
Independent Task Force Report No. 61 (2008)

U.S.-Latin America Relations: A New Direction for a New Reality
Charlene Barshefsky and James T. Hill, Chairs; Shannon O'Neil, Project Director
Independent Task Force Report No. 60 (2008)

U.S.-China Relations: An Affirmative Agenda, A Responsible Course
Carla A. Hills and Dennis C. Blair, Chairs; Frank Sampson Jannuzi, Project Director
Independent Task Force Report No. 59 (2007)

National Security Consequences of U.S. Oil Dependency
John Deutch and James R. Schlesinger, Chairs; David G. Victor, Project Director
Independent Task Force Report No. 58 (2006)

Russia's Wrong Direction: What the United States Can and Should Do
John Edwards and Jack Kemp, Chairs; Stephen Sestanovich, Project Director
Independent Task Force Report No. 57 (2006)

More than Humanitarianism: A Strategic U.S. Approach Toward Africa
Anthony Lake and Christine Todd Whitman, Chairs; Princeton N. Lyman and J. Stephen Morrison, Project Directors
Independent Task Force Report No. 56 (2006)

In the Wake of War: Improving Post-Conflict Capabilities
Samuel R. Berger and Brent Scowcroft, Chairs; William L. Nash, Project Director; Mona K. Sutphen, Deputy Director
Independent Task Force Report No. 55 (2005)

In Support of Arab Democracy: Why and How
Madeleine K. Albright and Vin Weber, Chairs; Steven A. Cook, Project Director
Independent Task Force Report No. 54 (2005)

Building a North American Community
John P. Manley, Pedro Aspe, and William F. Weld, Chairs; Thomas d'Aquino, Andrés Rozental, and Robert Pastor, Vice Chairs; Chappell H. Lawson, Project Director
Independent Task Force Report No. 53 (2005)

Iran: Time for a New Approach
Zbigniew Brzezinski and Robert M. Gates, Chairs; Suzanne Maloney, Project Director
Independent Task Force Report No. 52 (2004)

An Update on the Global Campaign Against Terrorist Financing
Maurice R. Greenberg, Chair; William F. Wechsler and Lee S. Wolosky, Project Directors
Independent Task Force Report No. 40B (Web-only release, 2004)

Renewing the Atlantic Partnership
Henry A. Kissinger and Lawrence H. Summers, Chairs; Charles A. Kupchan, Project Director
Independent Task Force Report No. 51 (2004)

Iraq: One Year After
Thomas R. Pickering and James R. Schlesinger, Chairs; Eric P. Schwartz, Project Consultant
Independent Task Force Report No. 43C (Web-only release, 2004)

Nonlethal Weapons and Capabilities
Paul X. Kelley and Graham Allison, Chairs; Richard L. Garwin, Project Director
Independent Task Force Report No. 50 (2004)

New Priorities in South Asia: U.S. Policy Toward India, Pakistan, and Afghanistan (Chairmen's Report)
Marshall Bouton, Nicholas Platt, and Frank G. Wisner, Chairs; Dennis Kux and Mahnaz Ispahani, Project Directors
Independent Task Force Report No. 49 (2003)
Cosponsored with the Asia Society

Finding America's Voice: A Strategy for Reinvigorating U.S. Public Diplomacy
Peter G. Peterson, Chair; Kathy Bloomgarden, Henry Grunwald, David E. Morey, and Shibley Telhami, Working Committee Chairs; Jennifer Sieg, Project Director; Sharon Herbstman, Project Coordinator
Independent Task Force Report No. 48 (2003)

Emergency Responders: Drastically Underfunded, Dangerously Unprepared
Warren B. Rudman, Chair; Richard A. Clarke, Senior Adviser; Jamie F. Metzl, Project Director
Independent Task Force Report No. 47 (2003)

Iraq: The Day After (Chairs' Update)
Thomas R. Pickering and James R. Schlesinger, Chairs; Eric P. Schwartz, Project Director
Independent Task Force Report No. 43B (Web-only release, 2003)

Burma: Time for Change
Mathea Falco, Chair
Independent Task Force Report No. 46 (2003)

Afghanistan: Are We Losing the Peace?
Marshall Bouton, Nicholas Platt, and Frank G. Wisner, Chairs; Dennis Kux and Mahnaz Ispahani, Project Directors
Chairman's Report of an Independent Task Force (2003)
Cosponsored with the Asia Society

Meeting the North Korean Nuclear Challenge
Morton I. Abramowitz and James T. Laney, Chairs; Eric Heginbotham, Project Director
Independent Task Force Report No. 45 (2003)

Chinese Military Power
Harold Brown, Chair; Joseph W. Prueher, Vice Chair; Adam Segal, Project Director
Independent Task Force Report No. 44 (2003)

Iraq: The Day After
Thomas R. Pickering and James R. Schlesinger, Chairs; Eric P. Schwartz, Project Director
Independent Task Force Report No. 43 (2003)

Threats to Democracy: Prevention and Response
Madeleine K. Albright and Bronislaw Geremek, Chairs; Morton H. Halperin, Director; Elizabeth Frawley Bagley, Associate Director
Independent Task Force Report No. 42 (2002)

America—Still Unprepared, Still in Danger
Gary Hart and Warren B. Rudman, Chairs; Stephen E. Flynn, Project Director
Independent Task Force Report No. 41 (2002)

Terrorist Financing
Maurice R. Greenberg, Chair; William F. Wechsler and Lee S. Wolosky, Project Directors
Independent Task Force Report No. 40 (2002)

Enhancing U.S. Leadership at the United Nations
David Dreier and Lee H. Hamilton, Chairs; Lee Feinstein and Adrian Karatnycky, Project Directors
Independent Task Force Report No. 39 (2002)
Cosponsored with Freedom House

Improving the U.S. Public Diplomacy Campaign in the War Against Terrorism
Carla A. Hills and Richard C. Holbrooke, Chairs; Charles G. Boyd, Project Director
Independent Task Force Report No. 38 (Web-only release, 2001)

Building Support for More Open Trade
Kenneth M. Duberstein and Robert E. Rubin, Chairs; Timothy F. Geithner, Project Director; Daniel R. Lucich, Deputy Project Director
Independent Task Force Report No. 37 (2001)

Beginning the Journey: China, the United States, and the WTO
Robert D. Hormats, Chair; Elizabeth Economy and Kevin Nealer, Project Directors
Independent Task Force Report No. 36 (2001)

Strategic Energy Policy Update
Edward L. Morse, Chair; Amy Myers Jaffe, Project Director
Independent Task Force Report No. 33B (2001)
Cosponsored with the James A. Baker III Institute for Public Policy of Rice University

Testing North Korea: The Next Stage in U.S. and ROK Policy
Morton I. Abramowitz and James T. Laney, Chairs; Robert A. Manning, Project Director
Independent Task Force Report No. 35 (2001)

The United States and Southeast Asia: A Policy Agenda for the New Administration
J. Robert Kerrey, Chair; Robert A. Manning, Project Director
Independent Task Force Report No. 34 (2001)

Strategic Energy Policy: Challenges for the 21st Century
Edward L. Morse, Chair; Amy Myers Jaffe, Project Director
Independent Task Force Report No. 33 (2001)
Cosponsored with the James A. Baker III Institute for Public Policy of Rice University

A Letter to the President and a Memorandum on U.S. Policy Toward Brazil
Stephen Robert, Chair; Kenneth Maxwell, Project Director
Independent Task Force Report No. 32 (2001)

State Department Reform
Frank C. Carlucci, Chair; Ian J. Brzezinski, Project Coordinator
Independent Task Force Report No. 31 (2001)
Cosponsored with the Center for Strategic and International Studies

U.S.-Cuban Relations in the 21st Century: A Follow-on Report
Bernard W. Aronson and William D. Rogers, Chairs; Julia Sweig and Walter Mead, Project Directors
Independent Task Force Report No. 30 (2000)

Toward Greater Peace and Security in Colombia: Forging a Constructive U.S. Policy
Bob Graham and Brent Scowcroft, Chairs; Michael Shifter, Project Director
Independent Task Force Report No. 29 (2000)
Cosponsored with the Inter-American Dialogue

Future Directions for U.S. Economic Policy Toward Japan
Laura D'Andrea Tyson, Chair; M. Diana Helweg Newton, Project Director
Independent Task Force Report No. 28 (2000)

First Steps Toward a Constructive U.S. Policy in Colombia
Bob Graham and Brent Scowcroft, Chairs; Michael Shifter, Project Director
Interim Report (2000)
Cosponsored with the Inter-American Dialogue

Promoting Sustainable Economies in the Balkans
Steven Rattner, Chair; Michael B.G. Froman, Project Director
Independent Task Force Report No. 27 (2000)

Non-Lethal Technologies: Progress and Prospects
Richard L. Garwin, Chair; W. Montague Winfield, Project Director
Independent Task Force Report No. 26 (1999)

Safeguarding Prosperity in a Global Financial System:
The Future International Financial Architecture
Carla A. Hills and Peter G. Peterson, Chairs; Morris Goldstein, Project Director
Independent Task Force Report No. 25 (1999)
Cosponsored with the International Institute for Economics

U.S. Policy Toward North Korea: Next Steps
Morton I. Abramowitz and James T. Laney, Chairs; Michael J. Green, Project Director
Independent Task Force Report No. 24 (1999)

Reconstructing the Balkans
Morton I. Abramowitz and Albert Fishlow, Chairs; Charles A. Kupchan, Project Director
Independent Task Force Report No. 23 (Web-only release, 1999)

Strengthening Palestinian Public Institutions
Michel Rocard, Chair; Henry Siegman, Project Director; Yezid Sayigh and Khalil Shikaki,
Principal Authors
Independent Task Force Report No. 22 (1999)

U.S. Policy Toward Northeastern Europe
Zbigniew Brzezinski, Chair; F. Stephen Larrabee, Project Director
Independent Task Force Report No. 21 (1999)

The Future of Transatlantic Relations
Robert D. Blackwill, Chair and Project Director
Independent Task Force Report No. 20 (1999)

U.S.-Cuban Relations in the 21st Century
Bernard W. Aronson and William D. Rogers, Chairs; Walter Russell Mead, Project Director
Independent Task Force Report No. 19 (1999)

After the Tests: U.S. Policy Toward India and Pakistan
Richard N. Haass and Morton H. Halperin, Chairs
Independent Task Force Report No. 18 (1998)
Cosponsored with the Brookings Institution

Managing Change on the Korean Peninsula
Morton I. Abramowitz and James T. Laney, Chairs; Michael J. Green, Project Director
Independent Task Force Report No. 17 (1998)

Promoting U.S. Economic Relations with Africa
Peggy Dulany and Frank Savage, Chairs; Salih Booker, Project Director
Independent Task Force Report No. 16 (1998)

U.S. Middle East Policy and the Peace Process
Henry Siegman, Project Coordinator
Independent Task Force Report No. 15 (1997)

Differentiated Containment: U.S. Policy Toward Iran and Iraq
Zbigniew Brzezinski and Brent Scowcroft, Chairs; Richard W. Murphy, Project Director
Independent Task Force Report No. 14 (1997)

Russia, Its Neighbors, and an Enlarging NATO
Richard G. Lugar, Chair; Victoria Nuland, Project Director
Independent Task Force Report No. 13 (1997)

Rethinking International Drug Control: New Directions for U.S. Policy
Mathea Falco, Chair
Independent Task Force Report No. 12 (1997)

Financing America's Leadership: Protecting American Interests and Promoting American Values
Mickey Edwards and Stephen J. Solarz, Chairs; Morton H. Halperin, Lawrence J. Korb,
and Richard M. Moose, Project Directors
Independent Task Force Report No. 11 (1997)
Cosponsored with the Brookings Institution

A New U.S. Policy Toward India and Pakistan
Richard N. Haass, Chair; Gideon Rose, Project Director
Independent Task Force Report No. 10 (1997)

Arms Control and the U.S.-Russian Relationship
Robert D. Blackwill, Chair and Author; Keith W. Dayton, Project Director
Independent Task Force Report No. 9 (1996)
Cosponsored with the Nixon Center for Peace and Freedom

American National Interest and the United Nations
George Soros, Chair
Independent Task Force Report No. 8 (1996)

Making Intelligence Smarter: The Future of U.S. Intelligence
Maurice R. Greenberg, Chair; Richard N. Haass, Project Director
Independent Task Force Report No. 7 (1996)

Lessons of the Mexican Peso Crisis
John C. Whitehead, Chair; Marie-Josée Kravis, Project Director
Independent Task Force Report No. 6 (1996)

Managing the Taiwan Issue: Key Is Better U.S. Relations with China
Stephen Friedman, Chair; Elizabeth Economy, Project Director
Independent Task Force Report No. 5 (1995)

Non-Lethal Technologies: Military Options and Implications
Malcolm H. Wiener, Chair
Independent Task Force Report No. 4 (1995)

Should NATO Expand?
Harold Brown, Chair; Charles A. Kupchan, Project Director
Independent Task Force Report No. 3 (1995)

Success or Sellout? The U.S.-North Korean Nuclear Accord
Kyung Won Kim and Nicholas Platt, Chairs; Richard N. Haass, Project Director
Independent Task Force Report No. 2 (1995)
Cosponsored with the Seoul Forum for International Affairs

Nuclear Proliferation: Confronting the New Challenges
Stephen J. Hadley, Chair; Mitchell B. Reiss, Project Director
Independent Task Force Report No. 1 (1995)

To purchase a printed copy, call the Brookings Institution Press: 800.537.5487.
Note: Task Force reports are available for download from CFR's website, www.cfr.org.
For more information, email publications@cfr.org.